"As an authoritative interpreter of the intercultural, Holliday has made yet another significant contribution, this time by autoethnographically interrogating the grand narrative of Orientalism juxtaposing it with native-speakerism. Cautioning against 'replacing one Othering with another,' he opens up 'creative diversity beyond large-culture fixity.' He has done so by combining the personal, the professional and the political, and more commendably, by de-centering himself as a researcher and intercultural traveler."

— *Professor-Emeritus B. Kumaravadivelu, San Jose State University, California, USA*

"Holliday provides a brilliantly honest and acutely observed intercultural auto-ethnography based on his journal of Iran in the 70s. The careful weaving of the personal with the theoretical traces the 'splintering' of grand narratives into the contingency and detail of everyday experience beautifully."

— *Cristina Ros i Solé, Goldsmiths, University of London, UK*

"Contesting Grand Narratives of the Intercultural offers timely and significant contributions that seek to unthink grant narratives through deCentred perspectives. Utilising a third-space methodology, Holliday foregrounds the politics of looking, the techniques of the body, the way in which we are perceived, and the attacks of cultural blocks that blind us to see threads of hybridity and takes us on a journey through thoughts, observations, reconstructed narratives, and deep personal reflections to demonstrate the (re)construction of culture on the go. We need this approach to un-learn, re-learn and co-learn so that we may develop open engagements and become responsive to unexpected hybridities."

— *Khawla Badwan, Senior Lecturer in TESOL and Applied Linguistics, Manchester ʾ... ʾan University, UK*

"Through an inveı  ng years in Iran, Adrian Holliday c about how the grand narratives of s from seeing so much hybridity wit osedly disparate bounded cultures. T ...ful and perceptive read."

— *Asef Bayat, Catherin & Bruce Bastian Professor of Global and Transnational Studies, University of Illinois, Urbana-Champaign, USA*

"Employing a thoughtful, balanced blend of theory and rich autoethnographic data, Holliday reflects on and analyzes his experiences during his years in Iran. His detailed observations are illuminating, his writing is engaging, and his analysis firmly counters the stereotypes and Othering embedded in essentialist grand narratives. This book is an important contribution to the study of the intercultural."

— Stephanie Vandrick, Professor, University of San Francisco, USA

Contesting Grand Narratives of the Intercultural

Contesting Grand Narratives of the Intercultural uses an autoethnographic account of the author's experience of living in Iran in the 1970s to demonstrate the constant struggle to prevent the intercultural from being dominated by essentialist grand narratives that falsely define us within separate, bounded national or civilisational cultures.

This book provides critical insight that:

- DeCentres how we encounter and research the intercultural by means of a third-space methodology
- Recovers the figurative, creative, flowing, and boundary-dissolving power of culture
- Recognises hybrid integration which enables us the choice and agency to be ourselves with others in intercultural settings
- Demonstrates how early native-speakerism pulls us back to essentialist large-culture blocks.

Aimed at students and researchers in applied linguistics, intercultural studies, sociology, and education, this volume shows how cultural difference in stories, personal space, language, practices, and values generates unexpected and transcendent threads of experience to which we can all relate within small culture formation on the go.

Adrian Holliday is a Professor of Applied Linguistics and Intercultural Education at Canterbury Christ Church University, UK.

Routledge Focus on Applied Linguistics

Making Sense of the Intercultural
Finding DeCentred Threads
Adrian Holliday and Sara Amadasi

Mobile Assisted Language Learning Across Educational Contexts
Edited by Valentina Morgana and Agnes Kukulska-Hulme

Complicity in Discourse and Practice
Jef Verschueren

Moving Beyond the Grammatical Syllabus
Practical Strategies for Content-Based Curriculum Design
Jason Martel

Contesting Grand Narratives of the Intercultural
Adrian Holliday

Sustainability of Blended Language Learning Programs
Technology Integration in English for Academic Purposes
Cynthia Nicholas Palikat and Paul Gruba

For more information about this series, please visit: https://www.routledge.com/Routledge-Focus-on-Applied-Linguistics/book-series/RFAL

Contesting Grand Narratives of the Intercultural

Adrian Holliday

Routledge
Taylor & Francis Group

LONDON AND NEW YORK

First published 2022
by Routledge
2 Park Square, Milton Park, Abingdon, Oxon OX14 4RN

and by Routledge
605 Third Avenue, New York, NY 10158

Routledge is an imprint of the Taylor & Francis Group, an informa business

© 2022 Adrian Holliday

British Library Cataloguing-in-Publication Data
A catalogue record for this book is available from the British Library

Library of Congress Cataloging-in-Publication Data
Names: Holliday, Adrian, author.
Title: Contesting grand narratives of the intercultural /
Adrian Holliday.
Description: Abingdon, Oxon ; New York, NY : Routledge,
2021. |
Series: Routledge focus on applied linguistics | Includes
bibliographical references and index.
Identifiers: LCCN 2021037910 (print) | LCCN 2021037911 (ebook) |
Subjects: LCSH: Intercultural communication—Iran. |
Multiculturalism—Iran. | Body-mind centering—Iran. |
Cultural competence—Iran. | Cross-cultural studies—Iran.
Classification: LCC HM1211 .H645 2021 (print) | LCC
HM1211 (ebook) | DDC 303.48/20955—dc23
LC record available at https://lccn.loc.gov/2021037910
LC ebook record available at https://lccn.loc.gov/2021037911

ISBN: 978-0-367-48299-2 (hbk)
ISBN: 978-1-032-18544-6 (pbk)
ISBN: 978-1-003-03917-4 (ebk)

DOI: 10.4324/9781003039174

Typeset in Times New Roman
by codeMantra

Contents

Preface

The purpose of this book is to use an autoethnography of my time in Iran in the 1970s to test my non-essentialist theory of the intercultural. The basic premise of the book is that our ability to see a more open, creative hybridity is blocked by established large-culture grand narratives of nation and civilisation. While these grand narratives can take many forms, I focus on the Orientalist grand narrative because it is arguably the basis of the common, neo-racist, picture of division between individualist Western and collectivist cultures of the East and South which also underpins native-speakerism.

My choice of my visit to Iran as a case study is because of its location at the beginning of my own professional development, at a moment of pre-native-speakerism, and prior to the globalised ease of communication that is often I believe falsely attributed to the blurring of large-culture boundaries – my thesis being that large-culture boundaries have always been imagined.

Contesting these false grand narratives of the intercultural requires:

- A deCentring of how we encounter and research the intercultural by means of a third-space methodology which attempts to put aside our large-culture thinking-as-usual
- A redefinition of the intercultural as *whenever* and *wherever* we encounter cultural practices and values that cause us to position and reposition ourselves
- A redefinition of culture as creative, flowing, boundary-dissolving, and changing – as practices and values that we can be inspired by and align our identities with, but which do not confine or define us
- Finding threads of hybridity that connect us through the normal ability of all of us to be many things

- A definition of (small) culture shock as caused by large-culture, Orientalist prejudices that inhibit finding threads of hybridity
- A recognition of hybrid integration which enables us the choice and agency to be ourselves in intercultural settings

Throughout, the third-space methodology employs an analytic autoethnography based on reconstructed autoethnographic accounts of my time in Iran. Placing these as separate instances of data enables me to stand back and reflect on myself as the analysand and on how they represent the continuing struggle between large-culture blocks and threads of hybridity in the transient process of small culture formation on the go.

Before embarking on this empirical part of the book, in Chapter 2, I attempt to deCentre myself as a researcher and intercultural traveller through an analysis of a discovered unconscious Orientalism in my upbringing. The empirical Chapters 3–7 analyse how I move away from initial experience of small culture shock to gradually finding threads of hybridity. This is a constant struggle through which an appreciation of how the people, practices, and values that I encounter by no means conform to the Orientalist myth of indolent collectivism. Instead, I find a world-claiming hybrid modernity and everyday cosmopolitanism. The scenarios in the empirical chapters move from personal space in streets and interiors, to personal management in catching shared taxis, to interrogating the impact of my Western presence, to finding myself in stories, media, and histories, to pre-native-speakerism as a block to understanding in classroom teaching and professionalism.

At the end of each chapter, I use my grammar of culture to map the changing nature of this struggle. At the core of the grammar is the recognition of how the experience in Iran draws from and contributes to my personal cultural trajectory. Interrogation of this trajectory enables a time travel of interconnected experience through past and present.

Therefore, while the title of the book, grand narratives, refers to a negative force, which will be the topic of the first two chapters, I hope that the rest of the book will be a highly positive read. Even where I speak about small culture shock, the power of the West, and pre-native-speakerism, the overall message is positive as I succeed in finding threads that enable me to connect with Iranian society in ways I had not previously imagined.

The book is not however about me and Iranian society *per se*. The six composite characters around which I build my reconstructed autoethnographic accounts, Mahnaz, Simin, Bahram, Bahman, Pirooz and Parvaneh, are Iranian but also represent people one encounters everywhere. Importantly, they have lives that transcend the imagined fixity of large-culture tropes. The way that they connect with my life before and after being in Iran represents how all of our lives before and after particular intercultural events can connect. My time in Iran is therefore a special experience that connects with and continues to be present in the special places to which I have been before and since.

Acknowledgements

I would like to thank fellow researchers, Katarzyna Gasiorowska, for introducing me to Thomas Ogden, Sarra Hiouani, Amina Kebabi, Ana McDermott, Ramzi Merabet, Amira Oukraf, Nour Souleh and Ismatul Zaharin for their brilliance and struggles to make sense of the intercultural. Chie Tsurii and Yasmine Sadoudi made specific comments on the text. My long-standing co-researcher, Sara Amadasi, shared ideas as a persistently reflexive, third-space, fellow intercultural traveller. Conversations with Alan Bainbridge, Jonathan Barnes, Claudia Borghetti, Dominic Busch, Haynes Collins, Alex Ding, Teti Dragas, Malcolm MacDonald, Yasemin Oral, Lina Rodriguez and Charles Williams made important contribution. Claudio Baraldi and colleagues in the European projects I was invited to were particular inspiration for the last chapter. Irene Melinu was invaluable in bringing me back to youthful vision and re-imagining the beginnings of intercultural travel. Thank you also to Mahshid Ghaem-Maghami for a contribution from the distant past, and to the Iranian English teachers who inspired me. Claire Margerison and Nadia Seemungal-Owen at Routledge helped brainstorm the initial proposal and final framing respectively. Mehri Honarbin-Holliday and Shabnam Holliday provided essential scholarship.

1   Distant places and everyday understandings

It continues to be commonly thought in the field of intercultural studies, in social science generally, and indeed in common popular perception, that the default way to think about culture is as large national or civilisational units – French, British, Western, Eastern – and that it is only because of recent globalisation, ease of global travel and communication, and the increase in migration that these default boundaries might be blurred. In this book, I will challenge this proposition and argue that the notion of separate, bounded, large cultures, each with their own distinct features, has *always* been imagined, inaccurate, and, moreover, a major barrier to how we can understand each other and a cause of prejudice.

I will maintain that this large-culture approach has acquired default recognition not because of science[1] but because of established Centre grand narratives of nation and civilisation. This has often been represented in popular and academic discourses by a separation between the West and the East with national and other large cultures as sub-sets.

Centre grand narratives

Centre implies dominant concepts that have taken on the position of defining the world (Hannerz 1991). Grand narratives of nation and civilisation are big stories that in many cases idealise 'us' and demonised

---

1 The science I refer to is the profiling of large cultures (Bolten 2014; Hofstede 2003; Lewis 2005; Triandis 1995), which can be traced to positivist, structural-functionalist social theory in which practices and values are functional parts of a social whole (Durkheim 1893/1964), which has contributed to an ideologically constructed methodological nationalism that prioritises nation in social research (Beck & Sznaider 2006; Holliday & MacDonald 2020).

DOI: 10.4324/9781003039174-1

'them'. That they are ideologically constructed is established in the postmodern turn (e.g. Anderson 2006a; Mannheim 1936; Mills 1959/1970; Schudson 1994).

The prime example that I will look at is the Orientalist grand narrative[2] which is presented by Edward Said (1978) as a Western reduction of the East, through art and literature, to false images of indolence. I will argue that it is Orientalism that has given rise to the established, false, large-culture trope that non-Western 'cultures' and all the people who 'live in them' are characterised by collectivist and high-context practices and values that inhibit independent thought and critically. I will also argue, as the book proceeds, that Orientalism has similarly given rise to native-speakerism.

This cultural labelling is far from neutral. It is neo-racist in that it reduces human groups to defining and confining characteristics.[3] Its political force is expressed by Jabri where she states that 'the culturalisation of the "other"' as 'only identifiable through tropes of cultural difference, exoticised, nativised, and forever determined by the signifying effects of culture' automatically increases the 'logocentric' power of the West in the sustained inscriptions of colonialism that are always 'viscerally felt' (2013: 11, 15). Its between-the-lines insidiousness is described by critical cosmopolitan sociologists (Beck & Sznaider 2006; Delanty 2012; Delanty, Wodak, & Jones 2008) in how this marginalisation of cultural realities hides beneath a veneer of apparently well-wishing patronage that pervades all walks of professional and personal life and makes symbolic violence look innocent.

Travel to Iran

To support my thesis, I will consider a particular case that does not come from the current era of enhanced trans-world communication

---

2 In a broader exploration of the nature of grand narratives related to nation and other communities, Anderson (2006a) takes us on an impressive tour of how sacred languages, histories, literature, industries, images of the conquered Other, language origin and so on were manipulated. Bragg's (2016) radio series constructs the identity of the British 'North around the grand narrative of industrial inventiveness, but then reminds us at the end that 'there's not one feature ... that, given time and a dictionary, I couldn't find in equal example in the South' and that 'Northernness, like the people, is a fiction' (citing interview with Colls).

3 A discussion about the relationship between cultural Othering and racism, even when 'unwitting', can be found in the report on the London street killing of a black teenager Stephen Lawrence (Macpherson 1999: 6.4, 6.17) and in Kubota and Lin (2006: 475), Spears (1999) and Hervick (2013), and in praise for culturally unexpected achievement (Flam & Bauzamy 2008; Wodak 2008).

and travel. I will use an analytic autoethnography of my journey to Iran in 1973 to test the proposition that culture, despite its huge diversity, has *always been* an open, creatively flowing phenomenon that does not define and confine us as essentially different to each other, until we are tempted, for a divisive ulterior motive, to imagine it not to be. My decision to focus on Orientalism is also because it has major relevance to the travel to Iran, as the East, and was what I found that I brought unconsciously from my upbringing, as will be detailed in Chapter 2.

At the age of 23, I travelled to Iran and lived there for six years. In the 1970s, this seemed the epitome of the extreme intercultural encounter at a time when there was no social media, international media coverage was small, and even international telephoning was difficult and prohibitively expensive. It was at the beginning of the era of Western youth travelling to discover the East. My purpose for travel to Iran was not, however, to experience the exotic, but to live and work there. My early-adult responsibilities of marriage, parenthood, household and career management and even learning to drive were very much formed there, with significant role models within my wider Iranian family, media, music, cinema, and so on. I give this detail to indicate that if there *was* to be evidence for 'Iranian, Eastern culture' to be essentially different to my own 'British Western culture', there was enough going on to demonstrate this.

The purpose is not only to test the proposition that essentialist large-culture boundaries are imagined. It is also to demonstrate that

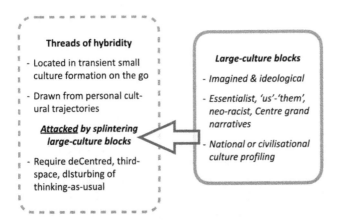

Figure 1 The ongoing struggle to find threads.

what can be found in a distant land in a distant time helps to make sense of the everyday intercultural here and now. As the book progresses, I see a constant struggle between threads of hybridity and large-culture blocks which I feel are present in any intercultural encounter. This is expressed in Figure 1.

Attack and struggle

I use the notion of blocks and threads to indicate what prevents and allows genuine intercultural understanding (Amadasi & Holliday 2017; Driscoll & Holliday 2019; Holliday & Amadasi 2020). The large-culture blocks on the right, within a solid line because of their dominant nature and apparent reality despite their imagined nature, literally attack the way that we look at people around us within the everyday process of small culture formation on the go, which I will describe below. The universality of this struggle is in the fact that divisive grand narratives are around us all the time in how we all spin, construct and reconstruct our images (Botting 1995; Goodson 2006) as they splinter into our personal narratives (Lyotard 1979: 22; Mannheim 1936: 52).

Here I wish to re-emphasise that the notion of struggle and attack implied in Figure 1 is paramount to understanding everything else. As the book progresses, it will become evident that the experience of Iran is indeed a battleground in which, chapter by chapter, the threads gradually prevail. The two sides of Figure 1 do not represent a choice between two equally valid images of the intercultural. The left side is where we *must* get to. The dotted border indicates that it is vulnerable to attack because the large-culture blocks will always appear more obvious and easier to understand. Kuhn's (1970) treatise on paradigm revolution helps us to understand why the illusion might seem to be the best choice. In his terms, the large-culture 'paradigm' will sustain because thousands of academics and university departments have based their careers and structures upon it (p. 151).

A developing theme through the chapters is that the battle of paradigms is, however, gradually being won. The hybrid intercultural reality that is revealed on the left side of the figure resonates with Stuart Hall's (1991) assertion about how cultural realities of the East and the South, that have been hidden and unrecognised by Centre, Western constructs, need to struggle to occupy Centre ground, and that indeed they are succeeding. Throughout the book, there is a gathering understanding of how the Iranians that I meet are claiming the world.

Of particular relevance here is Honarbin-Holliday's (2009) study of how Iranian women, from great aunts to university students claim this Centre ground through unrelenting personal action. This turning around of what used to be the Centre being claimed by what has been designated the Periphery resonates with Pennycook and Makoni's (2020: 7, citing Mignolo) assertion that "'decoloniality will no longer be identified with the 'Global South' but it will be in the interstices of a global order that was once divided into 'East' and 'West'"". The extreme nature of travel to distant Iran, therefore, brings out in sharp relief the issues that apply everywhere else.

Summary of chapters and data

In the rest of this chapter, I will look at the concepts listed on the left of the figure which enable the threads of hybridity to come into view. But first, I summarise what takes place in the ensuing chapters to provide context.

- **Chapter 2**, The Orientalist blocks I took with me

    - DeCentring myself as a researcher
    - Recalling the unconscious influences of Orientalism from education, childhood reading and media that I took with me to Iran
    - Imbibing the right to travel and educate the world

- **Chapter 3**, Small shock and finding personal space

    - Arriving, the railway station, the street, buying bread and home interior
    - Issues of personal space, order and function
    - Threads that pull from and contribute to my learning about personal space
    - Re-evaluating shock as lack of prior worldly experience and un-resolved preoccupations that I brought with me

- **Chapter 4**, Public spaces and hybrid modernity

    - Catching shared taxis
    - Hybrid and deCentred modernity pushing aside large-culture blocks

My empirical data is as follows:

- **Reconstructed autoethnographic accounts**. These are based on my memory of events that took place during my stay in Iran. References to particular people are anonymised through the use of reconstructed composite characters, e.g. Simin and Parvaneh in the above summaries. This is to avoid the identification of real people.
- **Artefacts** referred to in these accounts. These are: two English language textbooks, copies of which I have been able to access; a description of me teaching by an English language student; and several photographs of students in a class taken at the time. The textbooks are referenced according to normal academic convention. In all cases, analysis is by means of description which does not identify the particular people involved. The photographs are described rather than shown to protect identity.
- **Journal extracts**. These are taken from descriptions of events and locations which I wrote during the first years of my stay in Iran. They were pieces of creative writing rather than regular diary entries. The people referred to in these extracts are edited, again, to avoid identification of real people.

How this data was created and used within a constructivist, analytic autoethnography is discussed later in the chapter in the discussion of third-space methodology.

To protect identities, the reconstructed autoethnographic accounts are populated by a series of fictional characters who are composites of real people. There is also fictionalisation in some of the descriptions of places or events where this does not affect meaning or analysis. Here I borrow from my experience with creative non-fiction (Agar 1990; Holliday 2019: 55). In two places, I also reconstruct text from interview and email communication with an informant, Irene, who recently went from Italy to Japan in her mid-20s. I have made a decision not to refer to my personal family life except in passing. I have also decided not to talk about religion because I do not feel that it was pertinent to the analysis of the events that I describe except to refer to traditional or religious dress in public places which does not need more specification.

Threads of hybridity

I continue to be influenced by what I consider to be a major thread in Herrera's conclusion to her ethnography of a girls' school in Cairo:

It is Egypt, it is the East, it is also a developing country. But it is also humanity. Beyond my initial fascination with the exotic protocol, drills, sounds and system, it became just an ordinary school.... I cannot count the times I felt myself transformed over six thousand miles and more than a decade away to the parochial school in downtown San Francisco that I attended as a child.

(1992: 80–81)

One of the reasons that she may have come to this conclusion is that, despite 'initial fascination with the exotic', the major theme in her analysis is 'the lives, attitudes, struggles, relationships, confrontations, aspirations of ordinary teachers, students and administrators ... in a changing society' (p. 79) which could apply to any school, anywhere. This resonates with my first realisation of the concept of thread when I chose to speak to a colleague at a Chinese university about childcare, life-work balance and what it was like to be line managed instead of about the particularities of imagined 'Chinese culture' (Holliday 2016a; 2020: 34; Holliday & Amadasi 2020: 53). While there clearly are always practices and values that are particular to cultural contexts, there are also many other things going on that can bring us together. There is further discussion of this, where threads may become blocks in themselves in Chapter 6.

I am using hybridity as the qualifier for threads not to mean what I consider to be the more essentialist use as something in-between bounded cultures but in the sense of all of us being many things all the time.[4] Here I follow Homi Bhabha (1994: 56) and Stuart Hall (1996: 619) where they state that hybrid identities are the normal state of affairs and the nature of culture *per se* – as the nature of the cosmopolitan (Delanty 2006: 33). I therefore use 'hybrid' to replace 'non-essentialist' to emphasise that it is a positive, multifaceted power rather than a 'non' response to an essentialist norm.

Small cultures are not bounded places

There is an important implication here for the nature of small cultures. They could range from established social groupings such as a department, a social club or a family, to an event such as a meal or a meeting, or a chance conversation between two people in the street, or in a car. What I do not wish to imply however is that, for example, the Egyptian

---

4 A discussion of the essentialist and non-essentialist uses of hybridity can be found in Holliday (2019: 138, 146).

and American schools that Herrera is able to find connection between are bounded separate places like national cultures are imagined to be. While they had many cultural features that were specific to them, there would be many more that were not. When Herrera draws a thread of commonality between the Egyptian and American schools, this does not mean that there are two schools with essentially different cultures, because one is in Egypt and the other is in the United States. There will certainly be something distinctively Egyptian or American about them; but there will also be huge hybridity that connects them in multiple ways.

I feel it is important to make this point because there is a common, false view that cultures both large and small are a bit like places that define the values and practices of their members. The following two influential examples of this view are interesting because they seem at first sight to claim the opposite. While opposing 'segregation and fundamentalism' and preserving 'pluralism' and 'human rights' in its opening principles, UNESCO (2010: 3) states that 'culture should be regarded as the set of *distinctive* spiritual, material, intellectual and emotional features of society or a social group' (my emphasis). While stating that 'cultures are themselves multiple', Deardorff (2020: 4) states that '*each* culture is the sum of assumptions and practices shared by members of a group, *distinguishing* them from other groups' (my emphasis). This view would not allow Herrera to draw threads between Egyptian and American schools because they are in separate larger 'cultures'. Deardorff also refers to 'a nested series of progressively smaller groups' (p. 4) which invokes the seductively common onion-skin image of culture, where imagined essentially distinct features copy down into all their parts which in turn function to support the whole, within the structural-functional theory of society referred to above.

The dangerous implication of the structural-functionalist onion-skin model is that it allows the threads that are drawn between cultural realities only to be partial. It would be like saying that the Egyptian and American schools do have something in common *despite* belonging to essentially separate and different Egyptian and American cultures. This then falls back into the trap that can be seen in Lindholm and Mednick Myles's analysis of the international language classroom. Like UNESCO and Deardorff, they begin with statements about the hybrid and creative nature of culture (2017: 2) but then fall back to employing Western versus Eastern, individualism versus collectivism and high- versus low-context (p. 6) which then guide the rest of the book.

Therefore, no matter how small the culture we are talking about, its conceptualisation is still part of a large-culture approach as if it is considered to be an 'onion-skin' segment. I have referred elsewhere to this tendency to claim cultural diversity while maintaining large-culture boundaries as neo-essentialism (Holliday 2011) which may be a product of trying to find a recidivist middle way between positivist and postmodern positions, as referred to above with regard to Kuhn (Holliday & MacDonald 2020).

Defining culture and the intercultural

To counter this dominance of the large-culture approach in the field of intercultural studies, I therefore offer three definitions, of 'a culture' as a countable item, the intercultural, and culture in the figurative sense:

- **'A culture'** is something that we construct or imagine contingent on particular circumstances (e.g. as an operational setting to research, as a political or emotional rallying point, or as a branding or disciplining mechanism in organisations).

This definition, while maintaining that the notion of culture as a bounded place is always constructed, allows for the reality of this construction depending on what people are doing with it. Thus, we may cite particular values and practices that we claim 'belong' to 'our culture' as an act of resistance against political forces that threaten them.[5]

This does not, however, mean that we are defined and confined by what become idealised projections of these values and practices. The reference to branding and organisations in the definition helps here. An organisation might require its employees to behave in a particular way for the purpose of customer relations. It therefore defines and trains its employees in this (small) culture of behaviour, which involves

---

5 This relates to the debate between Cantle and Modood about multi-culturalism as related to minority groups in Britain. Modood rejects Cantle's suggestion for an 'interculturalism' that 'emphasise[s] interaction and exchange between a multiplicity of complex collective identities' on the basis that 'the national narrative can and ought to be inclusive of different cultural influences' and that 'undifferentiated collective identities as the basis for social cohesion, without a nuanced appreciation' of minority 'cultural identities' represents '"postmodern assimilation"' (Antonsich, Cantle, Modood, & Iacovino 2016: 489–490), and also to the notion of strategic essentialism attributed to Gayatree Spivak (Danius & Jonsson 1993).

forms of greeting, dress, demeanour and so on. The employees practice this culture while at work; but it does not confine or define who they are in the rest of their lives. There will however always be people who find it harder to deal with multiple cultural influences on their lives. The notion of subculture is helpful here, as discussed in Blackman and Kempson's (2017: 8) comment about members needing to be 'authentic' in their practices and values to be accepted by the group, implying that they have agency in how far they conform.

The reference to 'operational settings to research' will be picked up later in the chapter about third-space methodology.

An implication of the above definition's refusal to consider the reality of 'a culture' other than constructed is that the intercultural is *not* something that takes place between bounded large and small cultures. Instead:

- **The intercultural** as *whenever* and *wherever* we encounter cultural practices and values that cause us to position and reposition ourselves.

Practices and values could apply to a very large range of domains from what and how we eat, to how we deal with clients in business, to the style and arrangement of buildings and what is in them, to orientations in media and the arts. Thus, when we walk into a shop where there is a particular culture of employee behaviour and product display, we have to position ourselves – whether we approve and stay in the shop or leave because we do not like it. We do not imagine that the practices and values define and confine the people who work there or represent who they really are; and we may commiserate with them for also having to put up with it. There is a suggestion in Herrera's comment about schools above, that she is not saying the Egyptian one becomes familiar like the American one, but instead that the American one was also strange to her. Thus, intercultural encounters begin early in all our lives whether going to primary school for the first time or visiting the family next door (Holliday 2019: 18, 23).

The transience of the intercultural in the above definition is very clear when we are not attacked by large-culture grand narrative blocks. However, throughout the book, as I encounter and reflect on the memories of what happened in Iran, I need to work hard to pull myself back from falsely thinking that it is 'a culture' which is by its essentialist nature incompatible with my own.

I base the two definitions, of 'a culture' and the intercultural, on what Geertz says about 'culture' in a less countable sense:

As interworked systems of construable signs... culture is not a power, something to which social events, behaviours, institutions, or processes can causally be attributed; it is a context, something within which they can be intelligibly – that is thickly – described.

(1993: 14)

This sociological openness then opens up the restoration of the more creative a figurative use of the word 'culture':

- **Culture** is creative, flowing, boundary-dissolving and changing. It is something that we can be inspired by and align our identities with; but it does not confine or define us.

Hence, it is possible to talk about 'Iranian culture' as an open set of art, literature, architecture, music, cuisine, ways of eating, of greeting, of receiving guests, histories, stories, traditional dress, ways of walking, of touching and showing affection which do have something distinctive about them. It is also inspiring to the extent that people will align themselves and construct identities around it. There is undeniably something very distinctive and special about an Iranian music concert in London attended by a packed audience of clearly Iranian heritage people from all classes and religious inclination, brought together by something deeply rooted in their multiple histories. However, this does not determine, define and confine their behaviour in a structural manner that is essentially different to 'my British culture'. This concert is not defining the people there. Rather, for complex reasons of history and politics, they are *choosing*, at that particular moment, to define the concert and all the factors and references it brings together, as inspiringly representative of who they are. When I find myself there and open my consciousness I can find so many resonances in my own cultural background. At the age of 23, in London, before going to Iran, being at such a concert roused in me a powerful and inspiring sense of culture that I could relate to who I also was. As with Herrera's experience of the Egyptian school above, there was also so much about the concert that reminded me of other music events I had been to; and it was nowhere near as alien as the British football match I went to, where football was just not part of my life experience. There will also be many Iranians who would not identify with the concert.

My experiencing of and engagement with strange cultural practices and values in my time in Iran made me reposition myself and learn, not only how to live there, but also to reassess who I was and the cultural practices and values I had been brought up with. For example, strange home interiors and use of personal space in Chapter 3 made me re-align my assessment of diverse interiors and concepts of space I had previously experienced.

Small culture formation on the go

This process of searching for threads takes place within small culture formation on the go – the everyday location where people come together to engage with, make sense of and construct culture on a daily basis. Small cultures are any social arrangement where two or more people come together to make or negotiate culture. 'Small' is good because it is what can be observed and experienced directly. It is through direct observation that Centre grand narratives can be critiqued – what Stuart Hall (1991a, 35) refers to as needing 'to retell the story from the bottom up, instead of from the top down'.

Different to the process of sense-making in normative communities of practice (Wenger 2000), the working out of rules of behaviour in small culture formation on the go brings experience from far beyond the particular event. 'On the go' also implies dynamic trajectories which may involve choices about staying or leaving.

All my experience of passing through new locations, being a student then a teacher then married, and all the complexities of going to school, dealing with teachers, other children and lessons, making friends, avoiding bullying, dealing with the protocols of mealtimes at home, combatting teenage depression, and so on all come into play. Intercultural experience is then taken into the future. As I make sense again of the events in the autoethnographic accounts in the ensuing chapters, looking at them from a small-culture perspective enables me to see how they informed future action. Hence, in Chapter 4, I describe how catching taxis in Tehran contributed to my professionalism long after leaving Iran.

Personal cultural trajectories

The strong sense in small culture formation on the go of everyday intercultural problem-solving is both part of, informed by and contributing to personal cultural trajectories. At a number of points through the book, I make reference to experience of what I had done before and influence on what I did after – in Chapter 3, my existing anxiety about personal space and what I learnt about how to manage it in the future, in Chapter 4, the hitchhiking experience I brought to catching shared taxis and the primary research techniques I took on into my career. I make reference in Chapter 3 to believing that my generation was intensely independent of our parents, making up everything by ourselves and flouted all traditions. I was therefore very conscious of working out how to be with people and how to succeed in my personal and professional life. However, while arriving in Tehran was just a step up in this problem-solving process, it was the most foreign place I had been to; and I was desperate for clues for how to behave while maintaining my sense of Self.

Therefore, while I found these cultural appearances very different in Iran, my personal cultural trajectory had already exposed me to variety. I refer in Chapter 3 to how the strangeness of my friend's parents' home and how to be myself within it prepared me for differently structured interiors in Iran and enabled me to see a commonality of metastructure. Similarly, in Chapter 6, I refer to how my knowledge of television soap opera in Britain was a major route into learning language and the structures of family life through soap opera in Iran, where I also found familiar tropes of class, status and conflict. In both these examples, two very different instances of the same overall type are compared and hybridity within each type is revealed. At a certain level of generality, both the British and the Iranian soap operas are about family conflict related to class and status marked by outward shows of material possession.

However, small culture formation on the go is also vulnerable to the incessant attack from large-culture blocks. Hence the need for the hard work of a third-space methodology.

Third-space methodology

Searching for threads of hybridity also necessitates a third-space methodology – by which I mean entering into a thinking that steps out of the normal. However, while it is 'a place where normality is sufficiently disturbed to enable us to deCentre' (Holliday & Amadasi 2020: 8), it is also aspiring to be a normal space where 'new relations of self, other and world develop in the moments of openness' (Delanty 2006: 33). There is thus an aspiration for a new normality where the large-culture fictions on the right side of Figure 1 can be put aside. Homi Bhabha thus hopes that the third space 'entertains difference without an assumed or imposed hierarchy' by escaping the Centre 'fixity' of colonial discourse and 'politics of polarity' so that we can all 'emerge as others out of selves' (1994: 5, 94, 56). As with hybridity, the use of third space here is thus an important departure from a more common and essentialist use of the term that implies between bounded cultures both large and small.[6]

I find useful Soja's reference to third space[7] as 'a purposefully tentative and flexible term' which concerns 'the radical challenge to think differently' in a 'radical restructuring of long-established modes of knowledge formation' (1996: 3). His reference to expanding one's 'geographical imagination' (p. 3) connects with my recalling travel to Iran. His reference to 'journeys to "real-and-imagined" places' (p. 11) also resonates with our reference (Holliday & Amadasi 2020: 25–27) to Lalami's (2015) fiction about a 16th-century North African selling himself into slavery, being taken on a Spanish colonialist expedition to unexpectedly civilised pre-Columbian Texas, where he is captured, becomes a travelling doctor, and frees his oppressors. We see this fiction as a third-space device to help us see ourselves from a deCentred perspective – to remind us what 'what everyone knows' (as the threads we see around us every day) 'but no-one believes' (because of the attacking grand narratives that obscure this truth) (Holliday & Amadasi 2020: 30). I also find it significant that Soja finds it problematically uncomfortable that he 'chooses' bell hooks and her 'choosing marginality' as a position for analysis while he is an 'established and affluent, White Western Man liberally attaching himself, in the margins no less, to a radical woman of colour' (1996: 13). This resonates with how my questioning of myself as a Western visitor to Iran becomes a necessity in Chapter 5 but then trying to make sense of it through what I can glean as how I am seen by others.[8]

Especially resonant with the wider context of Iran, the notion of thirdness hints at a connection with that of the 'third script' as defined by 13th-century Persian mystic, Shams-e Tabrizi, in the following way:

> The scribe wrote in three scripts: one he could read but no-one else! The second both he and others could read. But the third neither he nor anyone else could read! That third is myself.
>
> (Saheb-e Zamani 1972, citing Shams-e Tabrizi, saying 56)

6 A discussion of the essentialist and non-essentialist uses of third space can be found in Holliday (2019: 138, 146).

7 Soja draws upon the work of Henri Lefebvre and Foucault; and he employs the capitalised form, 'Thirdspace'. He defines the three spaces as concerning (1) 'concrete materiality', (2) 'ideas about space', and (3) 'another mode of thinking' (1996: 10–11).

8 This trying hard to see from a deCentred perspective is also evident in Ros i Solé's (2019) use of Homi Bhabha's (1992: 141) concept of 'unhomely' as 'the estranging sense of the relocation of the home and the world', and in Badwan's (2021; 2020) direct observation of the personal details of the intercultural.

Shafak (2010: 19) tells us that Shams-e Tabrizi was 'a wandering der-vish with unconventional ways and heretical proclamations' who broke free of 'all conventional rules' in 'an age of deeply embedded bigotries and clashes'.

Looking back at my Western self and reverie

The points that Soja is making remind me that this book is not about Iran, or 'Iranian culture', but instead about how I as a traveller and researcher who is implicated in the particular, Orientalist, grand nar-rative that attempts to reduce the 'non-Western' world within which Iran and its people are situated, to an imagined image of cultural de-ficiency. This means that the autoethnography is not just a record of my intercultural time there, but a third-space methodological device to enable me to look at my own sense-making, and on what basis I can engage in the small-culture struggle to find deCentred threads. What I get from Shams-e Tabrizi is that this is very much to do with myself as a researcher and as an intercultural traveller, and the need to search inside my own reflexivity.

To enable me to stand back critically reflexively, I make use of an-other third-space concept. This is Ogden's (2004) 'the analytic third' – the possibility of unexpected thoughts arising from 'reverie' between the analyst and analysand in psychoanalysis. By problematising one-self as something set aside to be looked at, this then sets reverie in motion with the potential of new ideas wherever one looks. It is in this sense that the unfamiliar cultural environment serves to take one out of oneself sufficiently to shake the thinking-as-usual. I will come back to a discussion of thinking-as-usual in Chapter 4. Ogden's sug-gestion that 'the analytic experience occurs at the cusp of the past and the present, and involves a past that is being created anew' (2004: 178) helps me see the value of looking far into the past but also connect-ing my experiences there with what has happened before and since. Hence, my ability to see my stay in Iran as part of a longer personal cultural trajectory that also comes into the present. I have also written elsewhere about how developing intercultural awareness needs to time travel across multiple locations (Holliday 2016c).

That the analysis needs to be mediated with 'recognising the indi-viduality of the analysand' and also 'the analysand's recognition of the separate individuality of the analyst' through 'making use of their interpretations' (Ogden 2004: 191) also helps me, stretching the anal-ysand to both myself and the Iranian people I encounter as equally individual and hybrid, which is a major antidote to the Orientalist myth.

The notion of reverie in Ogden's methodology helps me to notice and see further validity in developing ideas and connections as I construct each chapter in the book. Each reconstructed autoethnographic account employs the ethnographic discipline of making the familiar strange and therefore takes on a life of its own. This forces me to think hard about what it means and connects with. As I juxtapose the elements in each account, the accounts before, relevant journal accounts, and the events before and after that they connect with, I feel myself being driven into the same sort of reverie as Matt as he searches into his past to make non-essentialist sense of the noisy woman on the train in Holliday and Amadasi (2020: 22–24).

Analytic autoethnography

This understand of the need to construct myself as an analysand influences the way in which I approach autoethnography. My approach is also first of all grounded in a constructivist ethnographic tradition that appreciates how both grand and personal narratives are socially if not ideologically constructed (Berger & Luckmann 1966/1979; Lyotard 1979). This acknowledges the inevitable implicatedness of how researchers co-construct what they and other people in the research setting think, do and say (Clifford & Marcus 1986). This brings both liberation and caution. The liberation allows an openness to whatever methodological device becomes appropriate. The caution is how I prevent an autoethnography of what took place more than 40 years ago from becoming indulgent anecdotes that simply confirm the ideas that I start with about highly imagined memories of a distant past?

I cannot therefore claim that the reconstructed autoethnographic accounts which are the mainstay of my empirical material are a true account of what actually happened. This is not just because they relate to events that took place more than 40 years ago. Even if the memory was from days after, it would still be my construction of what happened dependent on the narratives most influencing me at the time – a construction that would change from day to day. Even the few journal extracts which I wrote near to the time were constructions. Even if they had been written on the day of the events, they would still have been constructions influenced by other events. Indeed, the distance of 40 years enables a greater maturity of understanding of how these narratives operate, given that, since then, with a further ten years living and working in Syria then Egypt as an implicated Western English language curriculum developer, I began to understand the nature of the Orientalist grand narrative. There is also the danger that I am only talking about myself.

To address this danger it is useful to look at the discussion about whether autoethnography should be purely novelistic and evocative in its political agenda or be mediated by a separate analytic voice (e.g. Anderson 2006b; Atkinson 2006; Holman Jones 2005). My response is that it uses the same discipline as other forms of ethnography – making the familiar strange, referred to above, and allowing meaning to emerge beyond my immediate researcher agenda. Thus, while autoethnography brings the evocative meaning of personal experience, it is through looking critically at the personal experience of the researcher that meanings in the wider social world can be found (Ellis, Adams, & Bochner 2011).

The double eye and researcher voice

This sense-making and positioning and repositioning of involvement with the intercultural takes on a similar form whether we are explicitly researching or learning to live with a particular intercultural scenario.

This coming together of roles becomes evident to me as I work through the examples on the book with the double eye of having been there and now trying to make researcher sense of it. Whether or not one is a researcher, the positioning and repositioning that takes place in the intercultural encounter is embedded in the struggle between essentialist blocks and threads of hybridity.

Crucial here is employing a separate researcher voice with which to stand back and reflect on the other self of the analysand. Barnes (2014) mediates his autoethnography of his professional life with interviews with friends, his diaries and paintings, plus analysis of pieces of music that represented periods in his life, each of which enables him to stand beyond the predictability of his immediate viewpoint. Looking at and piecing together the exigencies of wider contextualisations of place, group, institution, and so on enables the crucial ethnographic discipline of thick description (Denzin 1994: 505; Geertz 1993: 6). This connects with Holman Jones's (2005: 770) reference to 'inventory' with respect to autoethnography. While *not* meaning large-culture national or civilisational profile, inventory means looking around and checking out things that one might not initially have thought of.

I therefore present the reconstructed autoethnographic accounts as separate texts with wider margins, as would be the case with interview or other data extracts. While there may sometimes be a fine distinction between these texts and further detail I present in the 'non-data' text, this separation of text enables me, and hopefully the reader, to see the difference between a recall of what happened and what I now want to say about it. It is a device to help me to manage the 'standing back'.

A final caution that a constructivist approach brings is that the concept of Orientalist grand narrative is itself no more than a construction. It is an operational or heuristic convenience – what Weber (1949/1968) refers to as an 'ideal type' – an idealised label that helps with sense-making. Prejudice and neo-racism are real in that we all really do reduce the foreign Other with 'us'-'them' stereotypes. I believe that this really did hinder me from finding threads of hybridity, and therefore caused small culture shock during my time in Iran. And I believe that this was indeed characterised by the imagination of the East described by Edward Said in his Orientalism thesis. However, calling this an Orientalist grand narrative is just a convenience; and I need to be open to it being something different. This book is not therefore intending to establish a definition of or reinforce the notion of an Orientalist grand narrative. I am using the concept to find out about something else – that there is an accessible hybridity in my experience in Iran that is sufficient to put aside any notion that Iran is a separate, essentialistically different large culture.

The grammar of culture

Figure 2 is my grammar of culture, which is a device for showing the different intersubjective forces acting on the intercultural.[9] The diagram represents the nature of the back and forth struggle between threads of hybridity and essentialist large-culture blocks. The blocks are indicated in italics as in Figure 1. Because I find this a useful template with which to see this struggle, I will bring it back at the end of the empirical Chapters 3–7, to help summarise the 'state of play' of this struggle.

Small culture formation and personal cultural trajectories (centre left and right) provide the experience and resources to help us forge threads of hybridity. Such resources also derive from the national and

---

9 The figure shows the most recent of a number of versions (e.g. Holliday 2011: 131; 2019: 2; Holliday & Amadasi 2020: 47). It is named after C Wright Mills' reference to what social scientists do to 'imagine and build' ideas and analysis as 'the very grammar of the sociological imagination' of the bigger picture of society and history (1959/1970: 234–235).

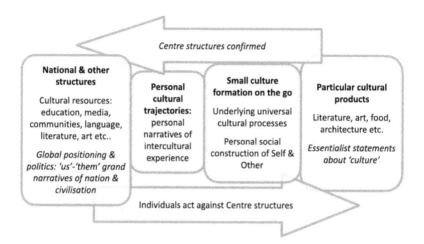

Figure 2 Grammar of culture.

other structures (left) which govern how we are brought up differently and provide diverse cultural richness. Examples of this are evident in Chapter 6, where my knowledge of the Anglo-Saxon poem *Beowulf* provides me with a way into making sense of the Iranian national poem *Shahnameh*. Similarly, particular cultural products in our different societies (right). However, the way these flow across national boundaries is evident in the Persian motifs found in British fabrics referred to earlier.

However, from these same domains come the essentialist large-culture blocks, where grand narrative serve how we are brought up to position ourselves globally (bottom left) and from the essentialist statements about culture we hear around us (bottom right) such as 'in my culture we think independently', implying *only* we, which, as the book progresses, will be seen as a clarion call for the Orientalist grand narrative.

This struggle against large-culture blocks is shown by the arrows at the top and the bottom of the figure, Centre structures being the national and other structures when they become large-culture blocks. The circularity of the grammar is in how everyday essentialist statements about culture (bottom right) confirm the globally positioning grand narratives (bottom left) from which they are splintered.

How far and how effectively individuals can act against Centre structures, which they both bring and find, in both newcomers and the people they meet, depends on political circumstances at all levels. I describe elsewhere how newcomer shop assistants are stopped by their employer from breaking the local cultural practice of not serving several customers at the same time, while young people in another setting use social media to help them succeed in introducing a new practice around paying the bill in restaurants (Holliday 2019: 170–171).

These might seem innocent examples with little impact on the political order. However, they indicate how small everyday action implies a dynamic image of society based on Max Weber's (1922/1964) social action theory. It opposes the crippling essentialist notion that people cannot think for themselves if they are brought up in totalitarian régimes. It takes small steps against an essentialist cultural relativism that patronisingly excuses acts against humanity because they belong to 'other cultures'. It is not 'my culture' that determines and excuses such acts. It is grand narratives about how people are and should be that splinter down to everyday régimes of cultural practice and can turn them into crimes against humanity. If people do choose to give up their autonomy to a grand narrative, they should be aware of the ideological nature of this choice.

2 The Orientalist blocks I took with me

Here I will look more closely at the nature of the particular large-culture blocks that I carried with me when I went to Iran and the nature of the 'us'-'them' grand narrative that attacked my ability to find threads of hybridity, as indicated in Figure 1. Already in Chapter 1, I have specified that this was Orientalist – a Western imagination of the East that reduces it to false images of cultural deficiency, as argued by Edward Said (1978).

I do however need to emphasise that this concept of Orientalist grand narrative is highly complex, difficult to define, and as the above list implies, seeps into other equally difficult concepts. It is based on my own reading of Orientalism[1] and what I personally see in the narratives, I have grown up with. It is not though just about me but all the people that I mis-imagined as a result. We all mis-imagine each other in varying degrees all the time.

I will now look at the elements of the Orientalist grand narrative that I took with me to Iran as blocks. This provides the contextualisation for what I would have had in my head as statements about 'my culture' and 'your culture'. Even though I was not aware of this academic politics of cultural description, I now realise that I had experienced the Orientalist grand narrative in a number of ways during my upbringing which led me to theorise about the Other that I encountered. Showing the degree to which the Orientalist grand narrative must have been present as potential explanation for what was going on in family, professional and other interpersonal encounters indicates how perceptions need to be shifted to arrive at the small-culture analysis of events in ensuing chapters.

---

1 A discussion of the critique of Orientalism can be found in Bernard Lewis (1982) and the reply by Edward Said and Oleg Grabar (1982).

DOI: 10.4324/9781003039174-2

Unaware despite reading

I was unaware not only that this grand narrative existed but of how it splintered into my everyday experience. This was even though I was, I believe, a deeply thinking and critical recent graduate of sociology who felt that he understood the ideological landscape. I had read and very consciously carried with me the critiques of grand narrative in, for example, C Wright Mills' *The sociological imagination* (1959/1970) and Karl Popper's two volumes, *The open society and its enemies* (1966a, 1966b). However, it might have been the case that I only applied these theories to what I tacitly thought of as 'Western society'. I will come back in Chapter 6 to Irving Goffman's worrying suggestion that his *Presentation of self in everyday life*, which I had also read, did not apply outside Western society (1959/1990: 236–237).

Just the fact of having read the theory does not mean that one applies it. This point is made strongly in Holliday and Amadasi (2020: 24) where ostensibly Western Matt needs to be jolted by his critical friend 'from elsewhere', Kati, into remembering all the critical postcolonial literature he has read on his master's course to help him understand his prejudices. The whole point about grand narratives as that are often between the lines of everyday life as are the discourses and ideologies that produce them (Wodak & Meyer 2015), so that we are often 'standardly unaware' of how we are implicated (Fairclough 1995: 36).

My informant, Irene, from her experience of working and studying in Italy, Japan, and France, tells me that people who live with cosmopolitan cultural flows do not realise it and explain their lives in terms of stereotypes or exceptions to them that colleagues unnecessarily construct behaviour blocks – e.g. about formal address – which they do not need to, and that students read about things like Orientalism but do not connect it with their personal experience – just finding it convenient to put both theories and people in separate boxes.

The following tour of the Orientalist grand narrative is not therefore of something obvious.[2] It is only many years after the events of the 1970s that I have been able to recover evidence of it. For this reason, as with my understanding of the nature of the events in Iran, I will set what I believe I experienced in my upbringing of the 1950s and 60s against later understandings. Hence, I am saying that I recognise what that was then because I have seen its development since.

---

2 A briefer discussion of the Orientalist grand narrative in everyday life can be found in Holliday (2011: 74ff).

This backwards and forwards referencing across diverse cultural scenarios and periods is part of the deCentred approach to interculturality through dissolved boundaries and therefore at the core of what we might call intercultural competence, if there is such a thing, as discussed in Holliday (2016c).

'The corrupt empire'

My first childhood memory to do with Iran was my mother's mild adoration of 'the Shah'. This was part of the same exotic imagery of distant and chivalrous male icons as 'King Hussein of Jordan' and the 'Sheikh' in the popular musical, *The desert song*.[3] While this was a period of iconic national leaders – Egyptian Nasser, Chinese Mao Tse Tung, French General deGaul, and Yugoslavian Marshall Tito, I remember that the Shah and King Hussein were different in that they inhabited the image of exotic, rich, and tasteful power. This romantic, colourful notion of power was also different to that of Napoleon, who I was in awe of in the final years of secondary school. While the Shah was somehow safe and modern because of oil, he was also associated with the imagery of the 'ancient, lumbering, corrupt and despotic' Persian empire that I had been led to believe in from school history – largely because of how it was framed as defeated by 'free and democratic' Greeks in the 5th century BC.

This stereotyping of the Greek versus Persian conflict in my education, the media, and children's literature ran throughout my upbringing and epitomised what I now know to be the Orientalist grand narrative. It helps me now to recall this when I see how it is present in the more recent film, *Alexander* (Stone 2004). Elsewhere (Holliday 2011: 76) I describe how in the film, we hear that the Persians are 'an inferior race', that the 'oriental races are known for their barbarity and their slavish devotion to their senses and excess in all things', that 'we Greeks are superior, we practice control of our senses, moderation', that 'the Persian soldiers do not fight for their homes but because this king tells them they must', that the Macedonians, in contrast, are 'free men', that Persian women may 'fool us with their beauty and degrade our souls', and that the Greeks are there to 'free the people of the world'.[4] I then watched again the 'epic film' that I saw as a child,

---

3 A YouTube link at https://www.youtube.com/watch?v=rrQ5Z1uqEFM shows a clip from the (1953) Hollywood movie.

4 It is beyond the scope of this book to get into a discussion of how far Stone intended to critique or was aware of the trope or to look at the layered complexities of

The ten commandments, in which the 'children of Israel' escape from slavery in Egypt. It has a similar corrupt empire, Orientalist message. In his on-stage introduction, the director, Cecil B DeMille, says that the film is:

> The story of the birth of freedom ... whether men are to be ruled by God's law or whether they are to be ruled by the whims of a dictator like [the Pharaoh] Rameses. Are men the property of the state or are they free souls under God. This same battle continues throughout the world today.[5]

In the final act of the film, the escaping slaves are tempted to return to the idolatry that is associated with the corrupt empire of Egypt which is resplendent with images of debauched, flailing women as they are lured back by the excesses of the evil empire.

'Exotic princesses and despots'

This representation of debauchery through the behaviour and appearance of women connects with the much written about exoticising of Eastern and North African women in Orientalist paintings of harems and baths (e.g. Kabbani 1986; Mernissi 2001). See also my analysis of the symbolic violence against Alicia and Roxana because of their 'extravagant' dress (Holliday 2019: 101–103). Elsewhere I describe how this Orientalist image, in my teenage years, was in the representation of Martian princesses in the novels of Edgar Rice Burroughs (Holliday 2011: 75) – exotically attired and in need of rescue from allegedly foreign patriarchies by the so-constructed white, Western, male hero. The resonance with familiar tropes in European fairy stories of princes, knights, and damsels reminds us that Orientalism is an exaggeration of a pervasive European fantasy. I did certainly, in the first years in Iran, construct theories about how women that I knew were defined and positioned by men – years before I was educated to understand that this was no more or less than in the West – helped immensely by the treatise on Iranian women by Honarbin-Holliday (2009) already referred to in Chapter 1.

---

ancient archaeological and modern media, historical and fictional representations of Alexander in Persia.

5 https://youtu.be/o8iNvzzak5U.

A powerful image on my secondary school syllabus was the unjust treatment of Desdemona by 'the lascivious Moor' in Shakespeare's *Othello* (act 1, scene 1). That the imagery of 'the Moor' was not critiqued indicated how well both teacher and students were unwittingly socialised into the Orientalist gaze. It also seemed normal to me that 'the Moor', alien emperor Ming in the *Flash Gordon* science-fiction television series (Worsley & von Fritsch 1954), and the 'summary executioner' in Henri Regnault's 1870 Orientalist painting[6] had similarly sculpted black beards, arched brows, and avariciously glinting eyes. Ming was often seen with women dressed in the common Orientalist image of the belly dancer[7] that also resonates throughout the science-fiction genre, for example, Princess Leia when imprisoned by Jabba the Hutt in the *Star wars: return of the Jedi* film (Lucas 1983).

A not so obvious but I think equally Orientalism Hollywood movie is *Independence day* (Emmerich 1996). There are no explicitly Orientalist images of people. However, the alien invader has the stereotypical weakness of being collectivist to the extent that the one who is captured expresses the intentions of the whole, and a virus delivered to the ruling core brings down the entire invasion force. This hive mentality of the evil empire is also seen in other alien powers in popular science fiction – the Borg[8] in the *Star trek* television series are ruled by a central, partly artificial, nervous system that disables any individual thinking. The Cylons in *Battlestar galactica* are similarly mechanical in their centralised thinking. Even when they produce multiple human-like forms their individualism is only an apparent deception. The images of collectivist evil empires do not so much demonise the East and South as idealise the Western heroes who are depicted as able to defeat them because of exaggerated and often eccentric individualism. However, they might be hugely dysfunctional in many aspects of their lives. Their clever bravery always wins out in the end.

'Doing the right thing'

I do not remember during my upbringing associating the corrupt empire idea with the British Empire. It did not feature formally on my school syllabus, and in childhood stories, it was only implied in

---

6 Musée d'Orsay, Paris, also referred to in Kabbani (1986: 77–78).
7 http://1.bp.blogspot.com/-EgVi1PfVU5o/URVg5xg_-WI/AAAAAAAARDo/ U6JBEKMbu4c/s1600/80038-050-EFC1B275.jpg.
8 Information about the Borg can be found at https://en.wikipedia.org/wiki/Borg.

positive images of boy and girl adventurers in foreign lands. When these stories graduated to more adult themes in Rider Haggard, they were about white male explorers in Africa, always imbued with honour and 'doing the right thing'. Their imperialist intent was framed as mutual respect through some sort of warrior camaraderie and understanding of what were really 'noble savages' – heroic characters dependent on the access provided by the 'white' adventurers to fight for independence against the imagined corrupt empires from which they came and were perhaps outcast from.

In school history and national mythology, this connected the small Greeks fighting huge empire with the idea of Protestant freedom versus oppressive Spanish Catholicism in the 16th century. The liberationist imagining of the British Empire and the narrative of the freedom of trade versus the imagined evil Chinese empire during the 19th-century Opium Wars is critiqued well in Amitav Ghosh's (2015) *Flood of fire*.

It is significant here to note that the Protestant work ethic was not only something that I was very aware of in my upbringing. This was not only through the direct influence from my parents in their seemingly relentless campaign against extravagance and waste and framing life as a steady ladder of personal achievement without a step out of place. I also read Max Weber's (1905/1950) *The protestant ethic and the spirit of capitalism* as a sociology student and began to see its influence everywhere around me, and certainly as the underpinning of the personal honour and 'doing the right thing' that I saw in my childhood adventure literature. Its implicit honesty code of always doing what you say and saying what you do was also to me a major antidote to the corrupt empire, as was the individual's personal contract with the divine without the clutter of intervening and hierarchal priesthood. However, my understanding or Protestantism was not at that time in the mode of critical analysis of an ideological grand narrative, but as a presentation of how the social order ought to be.

'My ancestors the ancient Greeks and the right to travel'

These notions of liberationist adventure, armed with a sense of Protestant morality, might well have been behind me feeling no fear and even a right to travel to Iran in 1973. I need to note this because this confidence was in stark contrast to wondering if I had any right at all when I returned there for the first time in 1998 after the 1979 revolution. Even though I was travelling for purely domestic reasons, on the plane I felt a deep guilt regarding my country's role as a post-imperialist power because of what I had learned in the years after the revolution – that it was now me who belonged to the corrupt empire.[9]

The origin of feeling a right to travel is also implicit in the *Alexander* film, cited above. The archetypal image of the philosopher Aristotle telling Alexander and his childhood friends to carry their simple morality into corrupt Persia resonates powerfully with my upbringing. The setting in which this conversation takes place in the film is a bare classroom which in itself is in opposition to the imagined corrupt lavishness of the Persian empire. Throughout secondary school, the ancient Greeks were presented as our ancestors.[10] My father taught me all the Greek myths and the *Iliad* and the *Odyssey*, which I read in my late teenage, were more important texts for me than the Bible, which I read as a comparable mythic text. One of my earliest memories from secondary school was taking turns to read aloud a story about the simple moral upbringing of children in ancient Sparta. I recently found that such stories from Plutarch still remain in an American study guide for school children (Carr 2017).[11]

This right to travel was then strengthened by the huge interest in the East that developed in the late 1960s. The Beatles were involved in Indian mysticism. My first experience of travel to a foreign country was to Germany, Italy, and Greece at the age of 20 with another student. We took with us the powerful Romantic narratives of German Beethoven, Italian Verdi, and Garibaldi, culminating in the image of Lord Byron fighting to liberate Greece from the imagined corrupt Ottoman empire at Missolonghi. This now seems a continuation of the 18th-century concept of Grand Tour to Europe by English Romantic poets and aristocrats. I recall the most totally 'foreign' experience being of the intense sunlight and shadows of Venetian streets, which somehow represented extravagance. Before our first ever experience of catching trains and planes, our preference was for the freedom of hitchhiking. It is again later that I see the iconic importance of this even beyond-the-world mode of travel made popular with *The hitchhiker's guide to*

---

9 One particular instance is the British role in overthrowing the democracy of Mosaddegh in 1953 to preserve their power over the oilfields (Borger 2020).

10 This relates to Gellner's (1964: 28) reference to the school syllabus in French colonies falsely including 'our ancestors the Gauls'. However, if, as suggested by Wu (2015), one perceives Europe in the same way as Europeans perceive China, as one consolidated place, referring to the ancient Greeks as my ancestors might not seem that strange.

11 A colleague from Serbia reported to me how similar texts about Sparta were used in Eastern Europe during Communist times to instil ideas of class conflict.

the galaxy (Adams 1979). This whole ethos of the right to travel with simple morality also resonates with a notion discovered many years later from the film, *Four feathers* (Kapur 2002),[12] in which the Sudanese Abou Fatma says 'you English walk too proudly on the Earth'.[13]

This right to travel is implicit in the international status of the so-labelled 'native speaker' English teacher which has been a major British and American export as a result of successful postcolonial branding from the mid-1960s (Phillipson 1992). There is indeed a hidden Orientalism in the native-speakerist ideology that continues to make this possible (Holliday 2005; Kubota & Lin 2009; Lowe 2020; Pennycook 1998). My travel to Iran was made easier by my easy employment as a teacher at the British Council. I did not realise at that moment that I was entering a profession that would provide rapid career progression that would make me a highly paid curriculum advisor at Damascus University, less academically qualified than my Syrian peers, at the age of 30. I will discuss the ambivalence of the status that my British Council teacher role carried, and more about native-speakerism in Chapter 7.

Nevertheless caution and positive images

It is not however the case that all imagination of the East was marred by false Orientalism. From late teenage I was reading Buddhist, Hindu and Taoist philosophies. It was within this trope that I located Edward Fitzgerald's *Rubaiyat of Omar Khayyam*, the 12th-century Persian poet, long before knowing about Iran. This literature influenced my worldview in a very positive and deeply philosophical and spiritual way. It increased my personal hybridity. Khayyam especially enabled me to feel a personal ownership of a route into understanding the very new historical and cultural references that I encountered in Iran. Neither was I alone in this. My reference, above, to the Beatles' interest in Eastern mysticism, represented a broad movement in the 1960s I think genuinely to broaden horizons. Neither was the influence of Khayyam new. In my edition of Fitzgerald's translation of Khayyam, the forward states that 'There is not a hill-post in India, nor a village in England' where it is not read, and that 'in America, he has an equal following' (1906: iv). One must also not deny the cultural contribution

---

12 This is based on the (1902) novel by A E W Mason which does not contain the same characterisation of the Abou Fatma character.

13 http://www.script-o-rama.com/movie_scripts/f/four-feathers-script-transcript-kapur.html.

of hundreds of British Empire civil servants who translated many volumes of Persian poetry into English.[14]

Therefore, while Khayyam enabled me to find a way into appreciating mediaeval Iranian poets, and while these were also of high importance to many Iranian people that I met, and were present in much modern cultural referencing, it would have been a gross and indeed Orientalist mistake to imagine that this was all that Iranian people were. I will look in Chapter 5 at how this sort of well-known mistake fuelled the ridiculing, which I often witnessed, at Western newcomers who thought they were integrating by dressing up in mediaeval 'ethnic' costume.

We are instead all hybrid

Returning to the theme of hybridity in the small-culture approach on the left of Figure 1, the evidence of the falsity of the Orientalist grand narrative that people 'outside the West' come from 'collectivist' or 'high-context cultures' that make them hierarchical, lacking in self-determination, autonomy and criticality, and generally devoid of the individualism that characterises the West is now emerging in a range of postcolonial sociology and critical applied linguistics literature. Honarbin-Holliday (2009) regarding Iranian women, along with a growing number of other studies of, for example Emirati, Chinese and Kuwaiti university students, Afghan women under Taliban rule, Italian children of migrants from South Asia, and minority ethnic Londoners, demonstrate that this is blatantly untrue (Amadasi 2020; Baumann 1996; Dervin 2011; Grimshaw 2007; Kamal 2015; Rostami-Povey 2007; Yamchi 2015). One might argue that all of these cases are exceptions to the large-culture rule; but this combatting of Centre definitions is also very evident in a vast postcolonial fiction (Mami 2014).

---

14 See *Encyclopaedia Iranica* entry, 'Great Britain x. Iranian studies in Britain, the Islamic period', https://www.iranicaonline.org/articles/great-britain-x.

3 Small culture shock and finding personal space

This chapter deals with what might be considered first-encounter shock, moving from the street to how the space around us is organised inside the home, in the arrangement and use of rooms, furniture, and eating, and how we share space with others and therefore the protocols for social engagement. While this might seem on the surface to represent cultural incompatibility, careful interrogation finds threads that resonate with experiences of unfamiliar spaces from childhood and early adulthood. These personal cultural trajectories and the narratives that accompany them are brought into play and take us into the future in our 'own' societies, where we benefit and indeed become culturally more reflexive and innovative from seeing the familiar as strange.

Revisiting culture shock

It is the notion of space and personal space that was perhaps the most culturally 'shocking' in that it is what first hit me as deeply unfamiliar. However, this, again, takes me back to early shocking moments in my childhood – going to primary school and the attachment to private space at home – and will therefore help to look at culture shock as an ongoing process through life that has to be dealt with in a constant manner rather than as a staged sequence towards what integration specific to living in a foreign 'culture' because of the difficulty of 'learning' and becoming 'acculturated' to an essentially separate large culture, as summarised by Furnham (2012). The *small* culture shock is therefore where, in making sense of the life around us, we are plagued by these grand narrative *blocks* and must struggle to search for *threads*.

When I now look at what I remember of the instances of shock, it was now to do with one culture looking at another but with a lack of

DOI: 10.4324/9781003039174-3

worldly experience that led me to suspicions that things were not meeting the Protestant ideal because of Orientalist indolence.

Efficiency and safety

The following is adapted from what I wrote near the time about the actual point of first arrival at Tehran railway station with a friend met during the journey.

> Eventually we got out of the station. There was a line of waiting taxi drivers and little orange taxis. Mahnaz approached one and began to bargain with him, asking him if he would use the meter. He threw his head up and clicked his tongue - 'tut'. So we lugged our luggage another fifty yards to wait in the street until a sympathetic taxi would appear. Eventually we found one and put our luggage on a precarious roof rack.
>
> (Journal extract)

Some of the language is quite threatened. This might seem like over-analysis; but I do remember how I thought at that time. 'Eventually' implies my framing of the experience of the railway station as the 'disorder' or 'pointless bureaucracy' that is associated with the collectivist corrupt empire. The same imagery applies to needing to bargain in opposition to my then imagination of Protestant straightness, as was what would have seemed exaggerated gestures that were associated with the South and the East. The fear of the efficiency and safety of the 'precarious' roof-rack then follows the now established construction that things were not being 'done properly'.

'Corrupt, dark and concealed'

This imagery of the exotic and indeed corrupt Other continues in my account at around the same of my first venture into the street at night:

> The dark streets were crowded with people. It was explained to me that most people in Tehran worked from about 7.30 to 12.00, and then from 4.00 to 7.30, using the hot afternoon to rest. The pavements were narrow and lined by young trees and deep ditches with running water between the trees and the streets. The houses and shops were side-by-side with no spaces in-between, like an irregular terrace, house doors onto the street, cut here and there by shop doorways and windows. Sometimes there were high house

walls which hid the house interiors and gardens from passers-by. Everywhere were flat rooves. Shrouded chadored[1] figures passed us by like ghosts, some pitch black, some paler blues and grey with tiny flowered designs. It made me tingle to actually hear the cry of the muezzin[2] – a shimmering, echoing cry which cut the air and penetrated every facet of the evening. Its difference to English church bells, a rounded booming sound which danced in the air and across meadows and on house rooves, signified the difference between the two cultures. The muezzin's cry was sharp but mellow, sad yet sweet, following a different, melancholic rhythm of life.

(Journal extract)

Here, the reference to dark streets is placed in opposition to lit modern streets. Years later this association between street lighting and modernity is emphasised in Andrić's (1995: 339–142) fictional account of the Austrian modernising of a Muslim town in former Yugoslavia, along with the straightening and widening of streets. My imagination at the time associated darkness, the shrouding of women and house interiors hidden by high walls, again, with the corrupt empire, where there are things to hide, in opposition to my notion of Protestant open honesty. There is a resonance here with an Italian colleague telling me that in an orientation session preparing her to visit Britain for the first time she was told to expect to be able to see into homes from the street because this was part of the Protestant need to let everyone see how they lived their lives. I remember my parents saying that you should not draw the curtains during the day because neighbours would think that you had something to hide. Indeed, Andrić describes how the street lighting enabled women for the first time ever to come out and promenade in safety (p. 142). While I had experience of terraced, or row houses, they were always regular and industrial, unlike the irregularity implied in the text. Even the reference to the afternoon siesta might have seemed to me to represent the Orientalist accusation of indolence – sleeping during the day when people should be working.

---

1 The chador common in Iran is a large piece of semi-circular cloth covering the whole body except for the face, hands, and lower legs, very often black when worn outdoors. It normally signifies more devout religion among some parts of the population.
2 Muezzin is the Farsi rendering of the Arabic for the person who recites the Muslim call to prayer.

What I had and had not yet seen 'before'

The visible running water at the side of the narrow street probably, at that first sight, seemed antiquated and perhaps unhygienic. At that time I was not yet aware that the street-side channels of running water were the product of the ancient Iranian major feat of engineering, the qanat system, that brought fresh water down from the mountains to irrigate fields and bring water into cities.[3]

However, I *was* familiar with the notion of the muezzin from the poetry of Omar Khayyam; and this, I think, brings a more positive note to the text where I compare a different but enticing imagery to that of English church bells, where 'shimmering' layers contrast with open 'meadows'. The sense of mystery here was more alluring than problematic. The reference to 'the two cultures' may have been figurative, inferring broad, creative flows, or may have been reference to an idea of two separate homogenous and essentialist places.

It needs to be noted here that these early descriptions were from someone who had not travelled far or extensively before. My two back-packing journeys to Europe had taken me only to a handful of foreign railway stations with little experience of catching taxis or bargaining. No internet and a far more limited repertoire of television and cinema also meant that I had seen relatively few images of places different to where I had been brought up – therefore making dark, narrow streets, irregular rows of houses, and covered women still a huge novelty. I am not suggesting that this made the Orientalist images described in Chapter 2 more powerful. I believe that the overwhelming richness of today's media simply serves to feed these images with richer examples to populate our suspicions about the corrupt and decadent Other.

Before the 'pizza revolution'

My query here about how much exposure I must have had is precipitated by the following description, from the same time, of buying fresh bread. Surely some of the strangeness expressed here would have been reduced had I had experience of how pizza is made in Italian restaurants – now commonplace in Britain. At the same time, it is clear that it is prejudice that gets in the way of seeing the familiar in the strange. The description of how one gets served, which is not

---

3 See the *Encyclopaedia Iranica* entry, Kāriz i. Terminology, https://www.iranicaonline.org/articles/kariz_1.

according to strict queuing, seems very resonant of what happens at the bar in British public houses.

> The bread shop was fronted by metal framed glass doors and windows, old and dingy looking. Inside was a group of people on an uneven stone floor. At a rickety metal table stood a peasant-like man in pyjamas and faded, shapeless vest,[4] taking money. Further in was an earthen kiln, built into the wall, into which a similarly dressed man was throwing dough, on the end of a long pole, which went right up into the fire and then spread across small pieces of red-hot stone. He worked like a maniac to an athletic rhythm. [There follows a detailed description of how the bread is made.]
>
> The bread was bought in twos, threes, fours and up to twenties by the people in the queue, piled and folded and put into newspaper or plastic tablecloth sheets, or plastic shopping bags, or just under a sleeved arm. Apparently the customers had to stand in the queue, which wasn't in fact a first-come-first-serve queue, and to try to attract the eye of the man who collected the money and give out the 'breads', and get him to take your money, which meant that you were near on the list for receiving. The trouble was that the man might be chatting to regulars or supervising the baking process, and didn't look your way.
>
> (Journal extract)

The focus on the 'rickety', 'dingy', and 'peasant-like' is therefore allowed to put into second place the skilled precision of the process and diminishes as haphazard the multiple techniques for carrying the very hot bread home. The reference to 'peasant' is coloured by my experience of a British industrialised agricultural economy that had already pushed the notion of manual labour on the land back to a feudal image of primitive subservience. The reference to pyjamas represents my confusion because of not yet having realised that what was worn in Britain as nightwear was actually brought from India where they were worn more widely.[5]

This was not therefore a culture shock brought about by a 'clash' of two incompatible bounded large cultures. It was instead the result of

---

4 'Vest' here is according to the British English usage, to mean a sleeveless undergarment.

5 'Pyjamas' was borrowed into English in the early 19th century from Hindi, itself borrowing from the Farsi word for leg garment – https://en.wikipedia.org/wiki/Pajamas.

prejudiced ignorance of the nature of a wider world of intercultural experience than I had before encountered.

A strange or just another home

In the following memories, there is a sign that threads are beginning to emerge as I find connections with my experience.

The following reconstructed autoethnographic account is of the first home interior I encountered. I focus on this because it indicates a bounded physical space of which I needed to make urgent sense. The first aspect of strangeness was the arrangement of the rooms and furniture:

> It was a first-floor apartment with a balcony that looked out over the garden of the apartment below. But most significantly, the rooms were all arranged differently to almost every home I had been to in Britain. Instead of a long hall, which connected the other rooms, front, back and kitchen and the staircase, the door let immediately into a large, central room which was the main living area and the centre of the apartment with bedrooms and kitchen directly off from it.
>
> There were familiar armchairs and sofa and a dining table to one end. However, instead of a fireplace around which the furniture was arranged to look at, the centrepiece was the carpet which filled the centre of the room and had hardly any furniture standing on it. Indeed, as I would later come to understand, the carpet was *the* major piece of furniture upon which it was common for members of the family and guests to sit and carry out tasks such as eating, reading and sewing, and generally relaxing.
>
> As, later, I visited other homes, I began to understand that, if means were restricted, the carpet was the most essential piece of furniture, preferred before chairs and tables, to allow a sense of home. Carpets were also taken on picnics as the basic place upon which to sit and eat.

This description is less threatened than the journal entries not just because it is written, as a reconstructed memory, at a calmer distance from the shock of arriving. It is also because I remember threads with other unfamiliar interiors I had encountered in my particular personal cultural trajectory.

The major thread was the *variety* of homes I had already experienced in Britain. My paternal grandmother's home was very different to that of my parents in terms of room arrangement and furnishing styles. Also, being a bungalow, with only a ground floor, it had a similar sense or room arrangement to single-floor apartments of which I had no prior experience. I had also lived in a wide variety of student accommodation. There was also, more recently, the friend's home I had visited in Britain upon which I based the reconstructed ethnographic account in Holliday (2019: 12). This had had the very unexpected arrangement of bedrooms downstairs and the sitting room upstairs. I had also lived in a variety of student accommodation which often defied all the rules of my childhood home.

There was also a major essentialist block. This was not so much to do with the arrangement and function of rooms and furnishings. Even the function of the Persian carpet as furniture was something that I remember taking in my stride. My generation of university students had been proud of our resistance to our parents' traditional use of furniture. Part of the influence of the 1960s embracing of exotic images of Eastern culture referred to in Chapter 2 was using the floor as a preferred place to sit. The Persian carpet concept therefore fitted well into my sense of 'alternative' living.

Function and ownership

The block that did sustain was instead me being anxious about the apparent lack of definition of the function of rooms, as the continuation of the description shows:

> The second major difference was the use of the rooms. The bedrooms seemed not to be 'owned' in the way that I was used to. While for most of the time each room was slept in by particular people, deviation from this was common. During siesta time in the afternoons, mattresses and quilts would be brought from other places so that all member of the family would sleep in the main living room on the floor - though not really on the floor, because the carpet was referred to as 'furniture'. On hot nights, the same arrangement was applied for sleeping on the balcony, even though it might let out from just one of the bedrooms, thus affecting the privacy of who was still sleeping in that room. Always, though, a carpet would be put down first to maintain the proper sense of 'furniture'.

This anxiety relates back to the Protestant desire for simple order as a mark of modernity. There is also the issue of privacy arising from not feeling secure in one's own bedroom, which I shall come to later. It is interesting that this anxiety also collects around the siesta, also referred to in the street description earlier in the chapter as connecting in my mind with the Orientalist image of indolence. In this reconstruction – and it is because I remember it so well that it is included there – it represented also an intensity of collectivism with everyone doing their siesta together, moreover, in a room that I did not feel was designed for that purpose. I believe that it was my feeling of opposition to this collectivism that led me to frame the afternoon siesta time as an enforced infringement on my 'individualist' rights.

Privacy, personal space, and eating

The issue of personal privacy seemed to sustain as the biggest block that developed from not knowing in which bedroom one could be secure from others. This is revealed in another journal extract:

> During the day, as there were no windows in the central living area, it was dark, and of course the coolest room in the house, like a cave out of the sun. The shower was next to the kitchen, a large, tiled room with a water heater and a washing machine in it. The shower was just a shower pipe fitted to the wall, with a tap built in. Although the room was large, it was difficult to find a place to put your clothes. There was a washbasin in the main living area where members of the family brushed their teeth with everyone watching.
>
> (Journal extract)

Again there is threatened language, though this time more subtle than in the previous journal entries. Insufficiency is revealed in '*no* windows', '*just* a shower pipe', '*difficult* to find' – and then the thought of 'everyone watching' what I considered to be private things like brushing teeth.

This perceived threat is also evident in this reconstructed autoethnographic account of how I perceived there to be a lack of respect for personal space at mealtimes. Again, as with the extracts about the bread shop and the interior above, it is to do also with a perceived disorder and lack of functionality:

> Then there was the business of sitting down to eat. There were no place settings. Instead of having that small portion of territory marked by a squared mat and knife, fork and spoon, it was more

like a sit-down buffet.[6] Everyone helped themselves from stacked plates and cutlery, and then from food in central dishes, and sat and ate where there was a space.[7]

The reference to place settings is to do with what I had considered to be my own rectangle of personal territory bounded neatly by table mat, and carefully positioned knife, fork, and spoon. The full colour of this discomfort is also expressed in another journal entry from near the time, where I make a direct reference to opposition with what I constructed as the essentialist norm:

> The first meal, the first evening and the first night were like an initiation ceremony which I failed dismally. It was about 8.30. There were strange smells coming from the kitchen that I hadn't smelt before. There was a lot of talk that I couldn't understand.
>
> There were no English table manners. Everyone sat down and helped themselves to everything. A spoon and fork were the tools, and the bread was used as a scoop. The plate was held at the edge of the central rice dish, and the rice scooped onto it, spilling here and there. I sat there dumbfounded, unable to move or speak, overcome by the deafening loud talk, arms reaching here and there, often in front of my nose, with what appeared to be incredible enthusiasm for the food.
>
> (Journal extract)

Again there is the threatened language seen in the other entries. 'Initiation ceremony' alludes to the sort of entry onto the barbaric tribes and civilisations that I had read in the childhood explorer stories referred to in Chapter 2. The sense of total disorder is enhanced by 'spilling' and the lack of proper tools marked by the use of bread as a 'scoop'. 'Helped themselves to everything' implies a breakdown of a morality of sharing. This was in direct opposition to my Protestant upbringing regarding eating where there was a strict observance of how much of what should be eaten, saved, and shared. This culminated in three basic rules at my family dinner table – never to take the last item on the central plate without checking if anyone else might want

---

6 A buffet is a mealtime event in which the guests take food from a central selection of dishes and then stand or sit where they can to eat, often going back for more.

7 This extract is adapted from my reconstructed ethnographic account, 'John abroad, politeness and space', which is also based on my time in Iran (Holliday 2019: 167) where there is further discussion.

it, never to eat anything unless properly balanced with the staples of bread or potatoes, never to have more food on the table than needed for the number of people present. All of this was compounded by the very physical discomfort with new tastes and textures plus a feeling of defeat and embarrassment at failing to behave appropriately as the extract continues:

> I had made a pathetically poor show of eating what was on my plate. I had never thought myself fussy and difficult to please at the dinner table; and now I felt like a spoilt child. I couldn't swallow it because it seemed too dry. The taste wasn't bad, but totally alien. I just could not eat my fill. I felt hungry but could not eat. My plate was removed; and everyone tried not to notice.
>
> After dinner came the fruit. The table was cleared of all else but dishes of all types of fruit. The father took on the role of putting choice pieces of fruit on the plates of the people there. All I could say was the Farsi phrase for 'no thank you', which I began to repeat, parrot-fashion whenever anyone tried to offer me anything.
>
> (Journal extract)

The feeling of loss of personal space was exacerbated by what seemed to be an esoteric sequence of events made worse by the lack of linguistic ability to participate.

Revealing hybrid contradictions in my own preoccupations

This anxiety about order, privacy, and function also however reveals the inconsistency in my *own* view of the world. At the same time as wishing to break away from the perceived strictures of my parents' generation's way of life by means of a more creative Eastern thinking, as described above, I feared the perceived decadence of the disorder that this might bring. This was therefore the nature of the small culture shock that I needed to come to terms with. Looking from the other side, my friend's parents, whose house had upstairs rooms downstairs and *vice versa*, referred to above, also thought that my 'good manners' were a sign of conformist, 'bourgeois' strictures. This worried me more because they were the very structures that I thought that I was trying to escape from.

This was by no means therefore a simple matter of my culture being just different to the Iranian one. There were complex small culture flows and inconsistencies that I brought with me, as there must have been in Iranian society and indeed in all societies. The following description of disdain about the association between modernity and functionality of rooms expressed by an elderly rural landowner in 1990s Pakistan indicates just such complexity:

Thoroughly disliking modern sofas, his heart still hankered after the palangs, the traditional luxury beds that graced living rooms in days gone by. The palangs, however, didn't go well with the rest of the modern drawing-room furnishings. They were being relegated to rooms labelled ostentatiously as 'bedrooms'.

(Shahraz 2013: 13)

I had arrived in an Iranian home without any knowledge of the probable history of conflicts about style and arrangement that culminated in the particular moment that I by chance of event observed, just as I did with my snapshot image of my friend's home in Britain. I did get a sense, on reflection about my friend's home in Britain, and as I got to know better the home in Iran, that in both homes there was an ongoing and conflictual discussion about how far they, and who within them, could claim to be 'avant guarde'. This is picked up in Chapter 6. This is the nature of the micro-politics behind the essentialist statements about culture, at the bottom right of the grammar, that we find ourselves making and that we hear from others.

Readers might therefore wonder if the Iranian home I describe is sufficiently representative. Were they 'real Iranians'? My counter to this is that in the ensuing years, I visited a significant number of Iranian homes. Most of them might be classified as middle class. They were all very different in the same way as middle-class homes in Britain are very different. This is simply evidence of the same degree in both societies of hybrid individualism, which I will say more about as the book progresses. A more appropriate question is why, if Iran is not the homogeneous, collectivist society that is imagined by the Orientalist grand narrative, we should even ask about whether or not a particular home is the same as others.

Finding new understandings about personal space

There were some practices that I would never get used to, such as group siestas, though probably. However, I began to realise that this was more to do with my particular personality – as someone who has always shied away from many forms of group behaviour in Britain. I nevertheless quickly got used to the new eating practices, tastes, and ingredients, this involved micro-practices such as holding bread in a particular way, eating with a spoon and fork, the rules that actually did exist for reaching, sharing, serving, asking, responding, and so on.

I also began to understand that my individualism was perhaps more likely to be given space in the social milieu that I became part of in Iran than I had experienced in Britain. The process of discovering the deeper rules of how this operated in this Iranian home made me also more sensitive to personal space everywhere than I had been before.

The reconstructed autoethnographic account moves on to show how this deeper understanding was precipitated by a particular event:

> It was sometime later, when the family were sitting around and talking, and Bahram turned round to me and said 'excuse my back', that I began to realise that, in this place where everyone seemed to sit so close that they were almost on top of each other, this was not after all a free-for-all and that personal space was as important as where I came from. It was something to do with this that conversations needed to begin with pleasantries. I had been told that I was being too invasive and abrupt when I wanted to begin every conversation with business.[8]

The reference here to opening conversations less abruptly will be looked at in Chapter 7. What appeared here to be a gentler awareness of the needs of others informed my behaviour years later:

> Even in work meetings I was conscious of considering the personal space of the people I was with – not turning my back, always at least thinking about what needed to be said before getting down to business. I had also learnt to understand that thinking that 'place settings' at mealtimes were all that were needed to ensure 'safe territory' was really very superficial.[9]

This carrying of what became an enhanced intercultural experience into life events long after the sojourn in Iran supports the back and forth notion of interculturality across time and space referred to throughout the book. The impact of everyday intercultural experience in Iran in my later professional life will be picked up in Chapter 4.

Another moment of realisation was in the following small event that I always remember:

8 Adapted from 'John abroad' (Holliday 2019: 167).
9 Adapted from 'John abroad' (Holliday 2019: 167).

A British newcomer complained to me about an apparent reluctance among his Iranian family to close doors at home. The poignancy of this was illustrated when he saw his father-in-law arrive home from work, go into his bedroom, which was just off the main sitting room, and proceed to change his clothes without closing the door. However, when he asked his wife why he didn't close the door for privacy, she replied, 'Why are you looking?'

This made me think for the first time in my life that private space does not have to be marked by a closed door.

These cited cases are not designed to establish the cultural norm in any given location. I am not intending to argue that, in Iran or Britain, privacy, or how we look at people has a clearly defined norm. There are people everywhere who will complain that they have no personal space, some of whom will claim that it is a Western value that does not exist in their environment, but others of whom will attribute it to family or other circumstantial factors such as social media, peer, parental or other pressures. It is how we can go about finding and being ourselves in whatever we might find culturally strange, that will help us to put aside racist grand narratives, that I am concerned with. What I am though arguing is that the more cultural variety we try to make sense of, the more creative we can be in working out how to behave wherever we are.

Applying the grammar

The way in which potential threads of hybridity are pushed aside by essentialist blocks, and *vice versa*, is very clear to me now. Applying the different domains of the grammar of culture helps me to understand this conflict. In Figure 3, I show this by populating the domains in Figure 2 with the particularities of what I have described in this chapter. As in the original figure, the items in italics represent the blocks, which are indeed present in all the domains. Two places are underlined to indicate that they have the potential for both blocks *and* threads. That the thread-block battle is being slowly won is indicated in the emerging ambivalence in the Centre structures in the top arrow, and the signs of challenge in the bottom arrow.

Thread-block battle

The core of activity is small culture formation on the go which, because of the dominant Orientalist grand narrative, begins with the

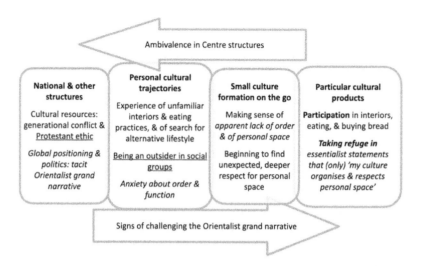

Figure 3 Grammar of culture (spaces).

blocking suspicion of lack of order and personal space, coming out of the station, walking in the streets, buying bread, and home environment. This is drawn from the global positioning and politics (bottom left) but also a personal history of anxiety about order and function before I went to Iran (bottom left centre). It is realised as a refuge in an essentialist view of 'my culture' when faced with strangeness (bottom right).

What enabled me to pull away from this blocking influence to find threads was the process of finding something deeper about personal space (bottom right centre). This was supported by experience in my trajectory, of the unfamiliar before going to Iran, which encourage me to search for something new (top left centre) and the resource of generational conflict in my own life (middle left).

Having been an outsider in social groups (left middle) could have maintained the essentialist block because it made it harder for me to join with the practices of eating and sleeping, making me fearful of loss of the safe territory of place settings and bedrooms. However, it also made me more appreciative of the sensitivity towards personal space when I began to find this. It also made me a more sensitive observer, as will be discussed in Chapter 4. The Protestant ethic (left centre) might seem the obvious block in its promotion of the imagined simple, honest, and organised Self in opposition to the imagined corrupt Orientalist empire. However, it also promotes the independence of mind that is necessary for direct observation and which seeks out and recognises the independence of mind eventually found in Iranian spaces.

Small cultures, third spaces, and shock

It is evident from the nature of the thread-block battle that the small-culture approach looks at what goes on in the mind of the newcomer when they encounter instances of culture. It is not trying to define those instances in terms of a cultural norm, for to do so would be to encourage large culture essentialism. However, visiting another family *even* next door can result in multiple interpretation choices, as I have described elsewhere (Holliday 2019: 24). The point here is that what is going on in settings in distant lands employs the same underlying universal cultural processes as in the local. Indeed, I also make the point elsewhere (Holliday & Amadasi 2020) that it sometimes takes being forced into more extreme unfamiliarity of distant lands that makes us arrive in the third spaced necessary to see beyond initial prejudices at home.

Looking again at the two arrows in Figure 3, the reference to Centre structures (top) is not to those in the society which is being arrived in, but rather to those that the traveller brings with them. The ambivalence is what was beginning to occur in my own certainty about the views I had brought with me which enabled me to see the unexpected and to deCentred my viewpoint. This automatically took me into the third space that is necessary to question Centre structures. Furthermore, this was not a highly conscious process. I was not aware of the Centre structures I was carrying with me. Part of the discomfort of the small culture shock that I was working through was what is part and parcel of the third-space process of questioning who I was in the face of new practices.

4 Public spaces and hybrid modernity

The slow emergence of threads of hybridity, as described in Chapter 3, led me to find more threads in my new life in Iran. It certainly helped to get out of the scrutiny of the home and into the hurly-burly of the street. The ideal location of this became travelling by communal taxi.

Taxis, individual space, and integrity

As well as going across the city and back to work, I was also travelling to multiple locations to give private English lessons to supplement my part-time employment at the British Council. Taxis were sufficiently inexpensive to be the mode of transport. I had rarely caught a taxi in Britain and been brought up to believe that it was an extravagant thing to do. It was my student experience of the liberation of hitchhiking, referred to in Chapter 2, that helped me to connect with the shared taxis practice. It too proved to be a liberating experience:

> To catch a taxi, one had to stand at the side of the road in the direction of travel and shout out the destination to passing taxis. Taxi drivers would be listening, also wishing to attract custom. They would stop if the direction matched that of other passengers already in the taxi. driver and passengers worked together within the communal use of space.

While, within the Orientalist grand narrative, this might have seemed a 'collectivist' experience, where the driver and passengers followed a traditional mode of established behaviour without too much thought for self-direction, it was actually very different. Neither was it a chaotic free-for-all. This is where I began to appreciate the care taken for individual space – within the confined and crowded space of the taxi.

DOI: 10.4324/9781003039174-4

The front passenger seat of the taxi, which was designed only for one person, would take two; and the gearstick was re-engineered to bend to allow them more space that wouldn't interfere with the driver. The driver took great care to monitor who sat where. If it was a female-male couple, the woman in the couple in the front had to be on the outside; and he would stop and have passengers get out and stand on the pavement so that they could get back in again so that women as far as possible would not have to sit next to men not related to them.

Everyone who got into the taxi was very clearly an individual, agentive person. This was therefore the beginning of finding an important thread – that people in this society were also organised just like 'us'.

At the age of 23, this was not just my basic training for catching taxis, but for other aspects of my still relatively new adult life. The respect for and the belief in the integrity of others that I saw in the taxis was transferred to my professional life.

Anonymity, strange, and familiar

My experience was importantly informed by making sense of observed detail. In the taxi environment, the ethnographic discipline of making the familiar strange was automatic. Travelling by taxi on a daily basis, with the forced necessity of succeeding in the multiple observational and communicative tasks that it required, became a highly focused study of the strange. While this was very clearly a very foreign intercultural environment, I began to acquire this strangeness as a normality so that it informed the familiar in the rest of my personal and indeed professional life. As interculturality is finding of Self in Other and *vice versa*, it is also finding the strange in the normal and *vice versa*. The anonymity of the street and taxi setting also enabled an outsider position within which to practise and make mistakes away from people that I knew where the interpersonal stakes were higher. I was also an 'insider' to a degree in the sense that any stranger getting into a taxi with other strangers is an insider. The fact that I was 'foreign' was of course undeniable.

However, one might query what it is that makes someone 'foreign'. One would need to talk to drivers and passengers about this. I was not at this stage able to read the foreign-or-not status of others as I am sure the drivers and other passengers could; but it was not long before I began to see the diversity and fractures within Iranian society with a glimpse of how it might seem through 'local' eyes. Some of this was in the brief conversations between the passengers themselves and the growing sense of how they read each other within the confined space of the taxi. Another was through television media that I began to be able to understand in stages – which I will look at in Chapter 6. One might argue that Tehran was not cosmopolitan in the same way as London – without the same number of tourists or minority ethnic communities. But this would also have been an illusion. Just because, purportedly, everyone was 'Iranian' and spoke Farsi, did not mean this. There had been massive migration to the capital since the 1930s, bringing 'multi-ethnicities and diverse' cultural perspectives, languages, and religious practices (Honarbin-Holliday 2009: 8).

Finding Self in multiple personal narratives of modernity

The communal taxi is an excellent reference for the concept of small culture formation on the go in that it was explicitly a transient inter-cultural space where people came and went and worked out how to be together in transit. While there was a common instrumental goal – for each person to get to their destination – and also for the taxi drivers to make their living, it was also a place of flux and sometimes dissent. There were indeed sometimes arguments that arose from differences of opinion between the passengers, but never to the extent of breaking the space and making it not possible to continue.

Also, everything that went on brought personal narratives from outside – from the personal cultural trajectories of each of the people passing through. Indeed, there was a considerable degree of recounting of these narratives as the passengers and the taxi driver shared glimpses of their stories. As a newcomer passenger, I also therefore got glimpses of wide and constantly varying snippets of Iranian life. The anonymity was a significant part of this.

One might argue that there was nothing particularly individualist or agentive about this and that it was a highly normative and collectivist community of practice in which everyone got on with a traditional mode. This would however very wrongly imply that all the people there were part of a homogeneous whole that did not need to be self-conscious about diverse identity. Albeit 40 years later, Honarbin-Holliday (2013: 61–62) speaks of an 'Iranian cosmopolitanism', which 'has developed organically and is plural, indigenous, widespread and intellectually fluid in nature' and 'accommodating ethnic, religious and class diversity'.

This goes back to the essentialist temptation that the foreign other is by default all the same and, in this Oriental case, therefore collectivist.

The point is that it was not just me who was an anonymous newcomer. I might have been less experienced at catching taxis than some of the passengers, but it is not an essentialist part of being 'Iranian' that one has this automatic experience. If this was the case, the driver would not need to work so hard to manage the situation. There was not just a wide diversity of experience but also of types of people.

Learning about labelling and hybridity

The passengers varied in class, age, provinciality, religion, politics, and so on, and they would probably be as busy with how they labelled each other as with how they labelled a newcomer such as me. As I began to learn the flux of their labelling of each other, such as 'up-town' and 'bazari', I found threads with my own preoccupations that I brought with me with whether men had long hair or 'conservative' short hair. Indeed, me making sense of the complexity of the narrative divisions in Iranian society might have softened my long-short hair block. Through this emersion in Iranian cultural life, I was learning about the complexities of labelling everywhere.

The passengers were also all going about their diverse business – hospital appointments, being late for work, visiting, escaping from family life, trying to work out how to get to unfamiliar parts of the city, and so on. At the same time, none of these identities were simple. Everyone was many things and therefore possessed the hybridity that would enable the negotiation of multiple threads.

This notion of everyday hybridity resonates with Bayat's (2008) notion of 'everyday cosmopolitanism' in which, despite the media's focus on the political élites of the Middle East:

> The ordinary members of different ethno-religious and cultural groupings mix, mingle, intensely interact, and share in values and practices – the cultures of food, fashion, language, and symbols – in history and memory. It signifies how such association and sharing affect the meaning of 'us' and 'them' and its dynamics, which in turn blurs and problematises the meaning of group boundaries.

The notion of passengers sharing stories and hybridities in taxis is also a theme in Iranian cinema. Two Iranian films, *Ten* (Kiarostami 2002) and *Taxi* (Panahi 2015) use the scenario of passengers getting in and out during a car and then a taxi journey to explore intense political and social issues that resonate with audiences across the world. Indeed, these film-makers were pursuing an agenda of revealing the multiple forms of everyday agency among ordinary Iranian people, and, therefore, breaking common Orientalist stereotype of indolent collectivism.

Diversity, agency, and deCentred modernity

Honarbin-Holliday also refers to these points about agency, professional management, and personal narratives of her daily interaction with taxi drivers on her way to her fieldwork site while doing her ethnography of two university art departments. Although 30 years later, her account resonates strongly with my own memory. She begins with describing the social phenomenon of shared taxis:

> Spaces on the move; seemingly a gap or a non-place departed from one point and not yet arrived at another. As they weave through the arteries of the city, the taxi drivers provide links, another socio-cultural perspective or political view, and oral social histories. I have looked upon these as metaphors, expressing transitions and much appreciated vernacular expressions from the heart of society.
>
> (Honarbin-Holliday 2009: 10)

She then recounts her own experience of the management and space dynamics as a passenger[1]:

> [I] sit next to two ladies at the back. The front seat is empty, so when the driver sees a man calling out 'straight ahead' he attempts to stop. It is difficult for him however to come to a complete halt because there is a chain of cars behind him. So he is forced to edge forward before the new passenger has opened the door fully to get in.
>
> Taxi driver to man getting in: 'I stopped for you, didn't you see me! I was holding up the traffic for you! You must be quick, jump in quickly, life is fast these days!'
>
> Passenger: 'No, I was not sure whether you were stopping or not. You were edging forward I thought. It's dangerous to just jump in, we have to hang on to these lives or ours despite the traffic! As a

---

1 These extracts and more discussion can also be found in Honarbin-Holliday (2005: 162–163).

matter of fact I have just returned from that eye hospital just up
the road.'

(2009: 48)

Honarbin-Holliday then describes how the man continues to recount
his experience with the hospital and how it is affecting his work, including speaking on his phone about it. She then continues to talk
about the two ladies sitting next to her:

> They are in their black chadors but I can catch their rosewater
> scent in the air. One says to the other: 'No I think you are mis-
> taken mother, she is going to do a degree in tourism now. She was
> going to do – what did you call it – a degree in 'trade insurance'
> before, but she has changed her mind. She thinks anything to do
> with insurance will ultimately be a world of desks and telephones,
> whereas tourism might actually have some travelling involved.
> Trade insurance. It does sound interesting, it could be connected
> to all this talk of globalisation. Can you believe it – you can do
> any degree you wish these days! A degree in trade insurance – it's
> marvellous!'

(2009: 48–49)

Honarbin-Holliday's final reflection on the conversation between the
two ladies is that, despite their 'black chadors', which many would imagine signify devout tradition, they 'could not be more contemporary
in their reflections about the choice of higher education available to
young people' and that 'you do not have to be Western to be modern'
(2009: 49). Indeed, throughout her book, she dwells a number of times
on the issue of modernity. I also, elsewhere (2011), pursue the evidence
for modernity not being the monopoly of the West.

Holding this idea of deCentred modernity firmly in one's head is an
absolute necessity if the Orientalist grand narrative is to be refuted.
The powerful implication here, that we need to keep reminding ourselves of, is that the Orientalist trope maintains that adherence to
collectivist traditions prevents the independent choices necessary for
modernity. In Honarbin-Holliday's account we see the refutation of
this assumption in the first passenger's explanation about why he chose
to catch the taxi, and the women's discussion of university courses despite their traditional religious dress. That Honarbin-Holliday herself
feels the need to continue to make reference to this implies her sense of
the unrecognised nature of the 'quiet march of self-realisation' of the
mainly female characters of her ethnography (2009: 165).

Honarbin-Holliday's mention of the women's 'rosewater scent' is also significant. While she does not use the term, this is a further indication of their hybridity. While rosewater is a traditional scent, it might not be expected of apparently devout women in public. One might say that it is just normal for traditional Iranian women to use rosewater scent; but even the traditional is by its nature hybrid. It moves and changes all the time.

Learning transferable skills from precise social processes

The urgency, anonymity, and shared sense of task within a bounded environment made the taxi an ideal laboratory for learning. There were located universals, a particular shared vocabulary and phraseology to do with describing destinations, negotiating them with others, giving directions about where to stop, suggesting and getting agreement about the fare based on calculation with the constantly running meter, the politeness of sitting next to others while protecting personal space, negotiating seating so that unrelated men and women did not sit together, which involved phrases related to gender, status, class, conversations about daily routines, and so on.

The language learning opportunity is clear. But here I want to look at how attention to specific and precise social processes in the highly professional setting of the shared taxi taught me other skills that I would take with me into my professional as well as personal trajectory throughout the rest of my life. This develops from my learning how to be sensitive to the personal space of others discussed in Chapter 3. It is important to note here that, at the age of 24, at the beginning of my career, my experience of professional engagement was brief. As well as learning something that I would apply again and again throughout my life, these were skills that I would carry into teaching, management, and research throughout my career.

Precise processes and porous small culture

The following is a recasting of the taxi catching experience which emphasises these social processes:

> In the street, there was opportunity to watch other people catching taxis and to learn from their demeanour, body language, tone of voice – how to shout and command without being presumptuous and irritating.

To catch a taxi, you had to shout the name of your destination with the right intonation and tone of voice to indicate certainty and authority while at the same time expressing respect. This involved very particular body language and gesture. Timing was also crucial. You had to meet the eyes of the driver just at the right moment, with the understanding that they were also looking out for customers and slowing down and pulling in nearer to the side of the road just sufficient to catch what might be called out.

When the taxi stopped, you then needed to say just enough more about the destination in such a way as to show the right degree of flexibility in consideration of the other passengers already in the taxi – leaning forward just the right amount not to crowd the driver and convince them that you would be the sort of passenger who would not upset the fine balances of the efficient impetus of the journey. The demeanour of your eye contact would therefore need to indicate the right amount of understanding of this necessity. Unlike, with tedious customers at the counter of a shop, with whom the shop assistant and other waiting customers would have to waste time, the taxi driver could, within seconds, decide you were not worth the effort and drive on without stopping.

Then, when getting into the confined space, you needed to say just the right few words of the right greeting, with the right body language and intonation to show due consideration for the other people there. This would be informed by rapid assessment of who they were on looking into the taxi at the same time as speaking to the driver.

And so on with the other practices throughout the journey and its completion. Much of this could be learnt from direct observation in the street, from inside the taxi looking out and inside the taxi.

This description is resonant of the 'needs analysis' (Munby 1978) with which I became familiar in the later part of my stay in Iran in my involvement with what became known as English for Specific Purposes. The idea was to define the precise language and its type of use required by a specific social setting. Who knows if my reading of this was unconsciously the more meaningful because of the everyday life experience of living and learning in Iran.

There is much merit in this level of detail. There is also relevance here to the points made in Chapter 1 about the nature of small culture. While the taxi may seem like a nicely bounded small culture, what was going on there also took in the side of the street where one stood to catch it and, indeed, the sides of all the streets where one might catch a taxi and all the taxis one might catch them. Furthermore, all the people there were constantly coming and going. Its smallness was fed by wider environments of experience, populated by the stories and histories we all brought to it. Very minimally, knowledge of the city and its locations was important – at the very least for *me* to know if the taxi driver's agreement to take me as a passenger was feasible and right. For all the people there, knowledge and experience of multiple occasions throughout their lives of how to interact with others. I perhaps need to reiterate that this was not our imagination of a collectivist national culture in which we imagine everyone automatically knows how to behave. Everyone there, including the driver, would be constantly assessing and reassessing how to position themselves with the other people there, and to varying degrees of success – just like anyone, anywhere in the world, would in such settings – practising the same underlying universal cultural processes that we all carry with us.

Transferable, third-space, intercultural processes

The elements of the processes I describe can therefore that can be transferred to other settings and tasks are:

- Direct observation
- Demeanour, body language and tone of voice
- Timing
- Eye contact
- Reading the intentions of others
- Precise delivery of relevant information and instruction
- The overall appraising of a social setting

All of these are interconnected and tightly paced to meet the needs of the setting. To demonstrate how these come together, let us look at a particular event from the account:

- To show due consideration for the other people there
- Informed by rapid assessment of who they were on looking into the taxi

This takes place at the moment in which I am about to get into the taxi after a rapid and successful interaction with the driver. What I see now is that there are similarities with what I would need to do on entering any social situation for the first, and indeed for the second and other times. This includes workplace settings. At that time in my life, these included entering the homes where I was giving private lessons, entering classrooms, meetings, and staffrooms at the British Council where I worked, and, a bit later on, entering organisations where I was doing outreach teaching. All of this was laying the groundwork for entering settings in institution management, curriculum development, and research later in my career, all of which needed to begin with rapid direct observation of behaviour.

The dynamic relationship between small culture formation on the go, the direct observation of particular social processes, and life, professional and research applications, is expressed in Figure 4. On the left is the positive outcome of small culture formation on the go, made possible by third-space direct observation which manages to see beyond the Orientalist grand narrative – for example, to see that this is not automatic collectivist behaviour. In the centre, the direct observation automatically employs ethnographic disciplines by virtue of the strangeness for the newcomer who has never before caught shared taxis in Iran or indeed anywhere. Is it is their prior intercultural experience of underlying universal cultural processes which however makes it possible to make sense of this strangeness. The figure is arranged in three parts to indicate that the encounter with particular social processes, no matter how apparently strange, or indeed not really strange, enables learning that can be carried into the future to take place.

The figure would also apply to all the other people in the taxi and standing at the side of the street catching taxis. What might be different between them is that there would be varying degrees of familiarity

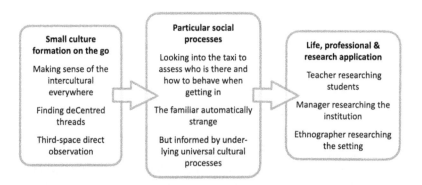

Figure 4 Learning transferable skills.

and routinisation that would drive these processes into degrees of 'what we do naturally'. It might however be surmised that more effective intercultural or communicative competence requires continued, conscious problem-solving attention to what is going on with other people – whether they be students in a classroom, colleagues in an organisation, members of your family, baristas, and other customers in a café or drivers and passengers in a shared taxi.

This is also a further indication that this is not about learning the rules of a bounded community of practice for the purpose of belonging to that community of practice, as referred to in Chapter 1, citing Wenger. It is instead about learning more about social life, to extend knowledge or underlying universal cultural processes – to further facilitate small culture formation on the go and the making sense of the intercultural everywhere.

Contributing to professional effectiveness

Connecting my intercultural experience of catching taxis with informing my later professionalism resonates with my interview study of Sara, an accomplished British Iranian administrator. She told me that she came to Britain at the age of 12 and found herself getting into trouble for engaging in what she perceived to be the Iranian cultural practice of explicitly watching people while in the lunch queue in her British secondary school:

> 'So I'd be looking at people's body language, the way they spoke to each other, their – just *general* observation. And I do remember *many* times being asked *what* am I looking at – very abruptly – and told to mind my own business – not that I'm *interfering* in anybody's business. So that was *one* thing I quickly had to learn *not* to do – simply *not* look at people because it was considered to be rude.'
>
> (Holliday 2012: 507, interview extract, her emphasis)

However, Sara traced success in her professional life back to this practice:

> 'It's something that comes naturally to me. I *learn* by observing people; and I've learnt many things by just *watching* other people – who do things in a particular way, whether it's presentations, whether it's just the way they deal with meeting situations, how they deal with people, how they communicate, their body language,

what*ever* it may be, that's how I personally learn. So I still *look*, I still *observe*, and I try and absorb it. ... One of the things that has helped me to *progress* in my career – watching people, learning, and, applying it.'

(p. 508, her emphasis)

Her referring to explicitly watching people as an Iranian cultural practice does not of course exclude it from being a practice in many other cultural environments. However, it does resonate with my own recollection which is exemplified in this event from my first years in Iran:

> I was for a short time hospitalised. I had a private room, but not in the same way as in a British hospital. It was expected that the patient's family bring food and generally look after them in the room. One day an Iranian visitor suggested we walk down the corridor for exercise. I was surprised when she stopped at the doorway of someone else's room and stood there for a moment to watch what was going on. When I showed my embarrassment and wanted to move on before the people there noticed we were looking, she said that it was embarrassing in Britain when people pretended not to be looking when in fact they were out of the corner of their eyes. She said that if you are going to look, you should do it properly and openly.

This has had an impact on my own consciousness in direct observation.

Negotiating cultural innovation

Like me moving from the initial shock regarding personal space to a deeper understanding in Chapter 3, Sara converts an initially discordant, apparently alien cultural practice, through working out what to do about it into a life-long project in a new country which also enabled her to be her Iranian self. For me, it was working out what is going on in the new place so that I could also be myself within it, but then finding that it can make me an improved self in future locations whether abroad or at home.

This sort of realisation is resonant with newer thinking regarding the experiences of so-labelled 'international students' studying abroad. Older thinking has been marred by the Orientalist trope of believing that students from the East and South need to learn how to be independent, critical, and so on through being in Western universities – ignoring anything of value that they bring with them. The newer thinking critiques this position as it begins to see that they do bring with them independence and criticality that makes huge contribution to global citizenship; but the struggles that they face in making sense need to be got to the bottom of.[2]

Looking back at Figure 4, it is indeed small culture formation on the go that is the basic site for these things to happen; but there also has to be something (on the left of the figure) to push us into third-space observation to find deCentred threads of hybridity. The basic ethnographic discipline of making the familiar strange (centre of the figure) is automatic because of the strange place we find ourselves in, and it is indeed then informed by our existing knowledge of underlying universal cultural processes. This might indeed depend on particular events that catch our attention and take us away from the apparent certainty Orientalist grand narrative. This was evident in noticing something different in someone saying 'excuse my back' in Chapter 3.

The significance of looking

As a further reflection on the politics of looking, Williams (2020), speaking about his attachment to the Venice Biennale, described how he and colleagues spent time in art galleries looking not just at the paintings but at the other people there also looking at paintings and each other. Mobile phones were an often-used device for this purpose, as some of Williams's paintings indicate. He also though reflected on an 18th-century fresco by Giandomenico Tiepolo – *Il mondo nuovo*[3] – *The new world* – in which Venetians are represented queuing to see the projected images from a camera obscura in a small building. I mention this to make the point that it is not just newcomers who experience the new even in everyday social settings. To imagine that the interculturally new and puzzling is only the domain of newcomers, especially Western newcomers, would be to deny the hybridity of all of us.

Direct observation, the stranger, and thinking-as-usual

I want to see if this notion of 'the hybridity of all of us' works with Alfred Schutz's notion of the stranger, which I have used in the past

---

2 There is a wide range of literature emerging that deals with these issues (e.g. Borghetti 2016; Caruana 2014; Caruana & Montgomery 2015; Dervin 2011; Grimshaw 2007; Jones 2017; Ploner & Jones 2019; Ryan & Louie 2007), including my own PhD students (Oukraf forthcoming; Sadoudi forthcoming; Souleh forthcoming; Wu 2021; Zaharin 2020).
3 Ca' Rezzonico, Venice, 1791.

as a basis for the beginnings of ethnography (Holliday 2016b: 9, 12). Schutz proposes that, on approaching a social group for the first time, in a sort phenomenology of arriving, the stranger does not share the thinking-as-usual of the people already there and has 'to place in question nearly everything that seems unquestionable' to them (1944: 502). Schutz says that thinking-as-usual 'includes the "of course" assumptions relevant to a particular social group' on the basis that 'social life will continue to be the same as it has been so far' on the basis of 'the knowledge handed down to us by parents, teachers, governments, traditions, habits, etc., even if we do not understand their origin and their real meaning', and of 'underlying basic assumptions' that are 'accepted and applied by our fellows' (p. 502, edited for gender reference).

I would like however, on the basis of the hybridity principle, to suggest that it might be a fallacy that any social group possesses a thinking-as-usual in the sense of some sort of conformity of thinking. It is perhaps at the core of how we Other the foreign everywhere to imagine that they are all 'thinking as usual' because of their imagined collectivist, unthinkingly traditional group thinking.

I would also like therefore to critique the notion that the stranger:

> lacks any status as a member of the social group they are about to join and is therefore unable to get a starting-point to take their bearings. They find themselves a border case outside the territory covered by the scheme of orientation current within the group.
>
> (Schutz 1944: 504, gender reference corrected)

In the shared taxi, even though I was a Western newcomer who had never had this experience before, I did have the status of being a customer and a member of the group of travellers, and I did have the ability, brought from previous intercultural life experience, albeit perhaps unconscious, to get a starting point to take my bearings.

'Lacks' is a word that I think should always be avoided because of its immediate sense of cultural deficit. Perhaps because I had learned to a degree of success how to behave, in many ways I was no more or less transient than the other people there. Indeed, as is the nature of small culture formation go, the 'scheme of orientation current within the group' was by its nature transient. While in all the taxis I travelled in I found a small culture of behaviour that was similar, all but the driver were transient, even though each of the passengers carried memory and experience of being in other taxis or, if this was their first time, they learned this from the experience of those who had.

I also therefore disagree with Schutz's suggestion that the stranger is 'no longer permitted to consider themselves as the centre of their social environment' and this fact causes again a dislocation of their contour lines of relevance' (1944: 504, gender reference corrected) because this denies the possibility that everyone in the setting can be both unsure and also able to find ways to be themselves.

One might say that the shared taxi is a very particular case in this respect. However, although I may not have realised this at the time, I cannot recall the experience of any social group where there is not some degree of transience. I am recalling now the family gatherings that I frequently attended at home. Even though everyone there was literally born into it, or had joined it through marriage, each individual, including children, was making their own sense with varying degrees of compliance. In all settings, the people 'already there' are making sense of how to be in highly individualist ways and that thinking-as-usual is very often far less complacent than it may seem. It is indeed the case, as with Sara introducing a more explicit practice of looking in professional settings, thinking-as-usual may be changed by newcomers.

This does not however mean that there would not commonly be essentialist statements about the culture which claim huge conformity to 'our culture' rules, which would be a major part of necessary feelings of solidarity. It might be argued that such statements are a strategy for dealing with transience, of manufacturing a sense of a 'scheme of orientation current within the group' (Schutz cited above) which might be less than imagined.

Schutz's suggestion that the stranger is not implicated in any thinking-as-usual also runs against the postmodern understanding, described in Chapter 1, that overturns the positivist notion of a distantly rational observer who looks from a distance at a virgin and unchanging culture by understanding the profound implicatedness of the observer and indeed the researcher.

Disturbing the thinking-as-usual

I feel that George Simmel's much earlier discussion of 'the stranger' is more supportive of an implicated newcomer and indeed researcher. He suggests that they are not so much a newcomer in a thinking-as-usual group – 'the wanderer who comes today and goes tomorrow' – but rather:

> The person who comes today and stays tomorrow... the *potential* wanderer... [whose] position in this group is determined, essentially, by the fact that they have not belonged to it from the

beginning [and] import qualities into it, which do not and cannot stem from the group itself. ... For, to be a stranger is naturally a very positive relation; it is a specific form of interaction.

(Simmel 1908/1950: 402, his emphasis, gender reference corrected)

Simmel also explains this positive relationship in a way that is resonant with the hybrid notion of interculturality:

The stranger is close to us, insofar as we feel between them and ourselves common features of a national, social, occupational, or generally human, nature. They are far from us, insofar as these common features extend beyond them or us, and connect us only because they connect a great many people.

(p. 405, gender reference corrected)

It also seems relevant here that Simmel positions himself within social theory against the structural-functional notion of 'a group mind' and for the idea of 'dynamic relations between individuals and in the interaction between individual minds' wherever they are able to 'enter into reciprocal relationships' (Martindale 1960: 237). His belief that conflict is a key part of social development (Simmel 1903) also runs against the idea of tightly functional group harmony.

It was true that, because I had not travelled by shared taxi anywhere before, my attention, as a 'stranger', was heightened and drawn to the precise details of how to enter that particular social situation. However, I think that this was a bringing to the surface and making conscious what we often do anyway. It employs the ethnographic discipline of making the familiar strange, and, indeed, making the strange familiar. This is to do with how we as people, and indeed as researchers position ourselves. We understand this as part of the implicatedness of the researcher as co-constructor within the postmodern paradigm described in Chapter 1, and it is a major theme of Holliday and Amadasi (2020).

My view is therefore that the disturbance is already present within the fibre of the social group and simply requires a little digging to bring it out. This observation brings fresh meaning to MacDougall's suggestion that 'digging necessarily disturbs the successive strata through which one passes to reach one's goal' and that 'culture is pervasive and expresses itself in all acts of human beings, whether they are responding to customary or extraordinary stimuli' and that 'the values of a society lie as much in its dreams as in the reality it has built' (1975:

121). This also implies that even essentialist statements about culture and indeed divisive and blocking grand narratives carry meaning and are as real to the people who even for a moment subscribe to them as alternative threads that connect them with others.

It is also important to note that all the people we meet in new places where we arrive (e.g. Iran) are also going through the same processes of small culture formation on the go, with their one personal cultural trajectories to make sense of us. Their national and other structures will in many ways be different to ours, but the use they make of them is similar. They also bring 'us'-'them' grand narratives that will prejudice how they look at us, as they do how we look at them. Indeed, these things also apply to how we all make sense of each other wherever we are. Other British people and other Iranian people will have different versions of these domains.

Applying the grammar

Figure 5 brings back the grammar of culture to make sense of the discussion in this chapter. Again, italics represent blocks at the bottom left and right of the figure: the Orientalist grand narrative, and the resulting default statement that only 'we Westerners' therefore respect

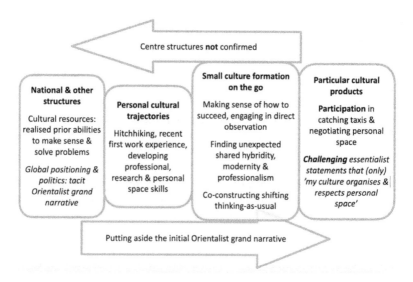

Figure 5 Grammar of culture (public spaces).

personal space. This is still there because this was my original hypothesis about the shared taxi – that my own personal space would be under attack in the 'crowded' interior. However, while the blocks are still there as potential inhibitors, the rest of the figure indicates that they are very much mediated by the other forces to which the chapter has drawn attention.

Hence, the top arrow indicates that Centre structures are not confirmed, and the bottom arrow that these have at least partially been put aside. This apparently positive outcome does however remind us that there is *always* negotiation with Centre structures. At the end of Chapter 2, I noted that it was the Centre structures I brought with me that are the problem.

Therefore, small culture formation on the go in this chapter is less about the initial shock seen in Chapter 3. Finding unexpected shared hybridity, modernity, and professionalism, that enabled co-construction of thinking-as-usual (centre right of the figure) was the significant breakthrough that led to *participation* on my own terms in the found cultural products rather than just being a foreigner looking on (middle right). These led me to new realisations of the positive nature of my cultural resources (middle left) and a personal cultural trajectory that was not just in the past but also far into the future (centre left).

This does not mean that the shock and blocks described in Chapter 3 do not continue. The persistence of blocking elements based on what I brought to my travel to Iran is taken up again in the next chapter.

5   Western newcomers

In Chapter 4 I gave the impression of Iran as an accessible society in which I was able to integrate on my own terms – being entirely myself and being accepted as such once I had worked out, through direct observation, how to behave, and had put aside Orientalist prejudices. There is however a major question that needs to be answered. Was this apparent ease of access because of my privileged position as a 'white', male, Western newcomer?

I have already said in Chapter 2 that the Orientalist grand narrative that pervaded my upbringing instilled in me a feeling of the right to travel. I distinctly remember the headmaster of my secondary school, in his speech to my class that graduated in 1968, telling us 'the world is your oyster'. While Tehran seemed economically better than Britain at that time, there was somehow no doubt in my mind that this was a temporary state of affairs. I will look at, in Chapter 7, how the clear Western ownership of the two key commodities of English and oil underpinned my professionalism.

Western positionality

That my awareness of this Western positionality continued to be ambivalent is evidenced in the following event which has often been on my mind:

> Bahman, who had spent ten years in the US, returned to Iran to live towards the end of my first year there. He was eight years my senior, had completed his studies with honours at an American university, and was already employed as a high-status engineer in Iran. As was common at a time when international travel was prohibitively expensive, he had not returned to Iran during that

DOI: 10.4324/9781003039174-5

ten years and was shocked by how much the city had expanded. He therefore shared with me the initial shock of being a newcomer. He was nevertheless also my role model. He represented to me the ultra modernity I found in many aspects of Iranian society that I had not at that time experienced in Britain. While I was influenced by the liberation of the 1960s, it was in him and his family that I first saw this acted out in domestic detail. His command of American English also seemed to me so faultless that for many years he was my model of American English.

It was therefore a great shock to me when, some months after we first met, he told me that I had no idea what it was like to be a newcomer in a country where one is considered to be inferior.

As was normal for students in the US, he had worked to pay for his university tuition. Bahman described briefly how, despite his good relations with friends, colleagues and teachers at the university, while working as a petrol station attendant he experienced racist abuse towards immigrants. Despite his modernity, his language and his evident ability to do whatever task was given to him with a high degree of competence, there was something about his appearance that didn't allow him to pass in this manual role in what appeared to be a highly multicultural society.

Despite all the Orientalism implicit in my upbringing, and having been knowledgeable of the Black Power movement in the United States, of Apartheid in South Africa, and the then relatively recent Holocaust in Europe, having heard my parents and their friends complain about South Asian migrants, having had Black and Asian friends as a student, having worked as a hospital porter during the university vacation in a northern multicultural city, this was the first time I ever met someone who spoke about personal experience of racism. Since that time, I have met a number of long-term Iranian residents in Britain, all highly successful in the business and academic sectors, who have told me how they have had to 'put up' with subtle yet persistent racism. The phrase 'people who look like me with my sort of name' is now well-known. Kebabi's (forthcoming) study of current university academics who 'come from outside Britain', including from southern Europe, shows how often their identities are under attack despite their high middle-class status.

This therefore begs the question of whether or not integrating with whatever aspect of Iranian society I chose was just too easy because of my indisputable male Western whiteness, to which I think I must add so-labelled 'native' English-speaking. In each of these highly contestable clearly ideologically and racially motivated categories, I was an easy if not obvious member.

'Chose' might be too strong a term. Through marriage I was embedded in an Iranian family. To make a living I travelled around the city by taxi and went to people's homes to give private English lessons. For our first apartment, I had to deal with the people we were renting from. I did however choose to take a deep interest in popular, modern and classical music, cinema, television, history and the media that was available to me, as I will describe in Chapter 6. These choices may have been due to what was available to me at a time when there was not the access that newcomers today have to the worlds that they have travelled from through the internet and social media. While there were a few international bookshops and the beginnings of an audio-cassette industry, I did not read the European sociology or philosophy, or listen to the European classical music that I had previously been interested in for several years after arrival.

Demeanour and sincerity

This does not however mean that I did not have difficulties with being accepted during my first six months. While these were not for racist reasons, they were I think to do with my presence as a Western newcomer. I say they were not racist because this never occurred to me. Also, I became quite quickly aware of other reasons for an apparent initial rejection of my presence.

One instance was my recollection of how I was received in a local shop:

> There was a small shop at the end of the street where I lived where I would go every day to buy basic groceries. There was not, for me, a recognisable method for being served in turn. There were never more than four or five people waiting to be served and the space for waiting was sufficiently small for everyone to be seen by the shopkeeper. However, for the first six months I found it very hard to get served until all the other customers had left, despite being a very regular customer. Then, very suddenly, without warning, I managed. It may have been something to do with making the right sort of eye contact or having the right body language. It was not a matter of waiting in line but of somehow being recognised.

I felt at the time that a significant point here was that my not being served was short-lived; and I never had this sort of difficulty again during my six-year sojourn or any of my later visits to Iran. My associating this difficulty with eye contact and body language connects with a second memory of just being in the street:

At about the same time of suddenly getting served in the shop, my physical presence in the street became easier. For the first six months I had difficulty walking among other people. They did not sense my presence when I walked up behind them, making it hard for me to get past. I was constantly bumping into people. I also had difficulty crossing busy roads. It was the norm to walk amongst the traffic while crossing; but it took me a long time to work out how to do this. I eventually learnt that the key was to make eye contact with oncoming drivers; but it was also a lot to do with body language – small hand signals to the drivers. At the beginning, even when crossing at lights when the traffic was stopped, some drivers would seem to lurch forward as though feigning being about to run me over. This seemed also partly to do with motor skills. In the first week in Tehran, my finger nails were always getting dirty and my clothes dusty. I had beige trousers that became filthy after a couple of days. Clearly I was touching and rubbing against things because of my clumsiness with the physical environment. This is resonant with small children who have not yet learnt to negotiate their larger environment, touching windows, walls, shelves and so on in such a way that their hands and knees are always dirty.

This description represents a strong awareness that I had at the time and which I recall vividly. However, I do not think that body language here is about what has been referred to as kinesics, expressing 'thoughts, feelings, moods, intentions, and/or attitudes and may be used in combination with, or instead of, verbal communication' (Padula 2009: 582). It is more like what Mauss (1973/1935) refers to as 'techniques of the body' to do with walking, standing, sitting, eating, arm and leg movements, and so on, which are specific to particular societies, age, gender, or other groups, but which can be learned by newcomers. Such techniques can be very small things like using the fourth, little finger, instead of the first, forefinger, to indicate 'one', washing the face by pulling water down it with the stretched-out thumb and forefinger. They might be considered arbitrary in the sense that they do not convey conscious meaning.

At another level, slightly less arbitrary, are movements that are somehow locked into more conscious cultural behaviour in the area of proxemics. During my doctoral research in Egyptian universities

I noted as 'culturally different' how, when coming into an empty class-room, rather than spreading out into the larger space, students would choose to sit as close as possible to someone already there, even moving the person's bag on the seat next to them to do so. I also noted that they were able to listen and respond to what the lecturer was saying at the same time as talking amongst themselves (Holliday 1994: 56).

However, very importantly, more life experience since that time has shown me significantly different proxemic behaviour among different age and other small culture groups within what might be defined as 'my own society'. Equally 'strange' to me is the extreme physicality of a group of young women British students choosing to share the same seats in the campus waiting area. I also marvel at how my own grandchildren are able to multi-task between simultaneous, intensely preoccupied play and responding to the wider social environment.

The broader point I therefore wish to make here is that, wherever one looks, there are very small and bigger micro-aspects of cultural behaviour that are on the one hand specific to particular social groups while on the other dynamic, in constant flux, able to cross imagined cultural boundaries, and entirely learnable by newcomers, while forgettable by longer-term members. They do not represent any form of culture-locked, essentialist value systems, and newcomers can learn them without any 'loss of their own culture'.

Projecting cultural exclusivity

What is more probable is that for different reasons and at different times, we feel the need to project cultural exclusivity. This is the basis for essentialist statements about culture as expressed in the bottom right of the grammar of culture. Being a newcomer in a strange society would certainly encourage such 'us'-'them' thinking. This point is made well by the example of a British English teacher standing at a bus stop in Hong Kong and being annoyed by students asking her where she is going (Spencer-Oatey 2000: 1). It seems that the teacher interprets this as behaviour from a different culture and therefore as some sort of invasion of her privacy according to her 'British culture'. In my experience of standing at bus stops in Britain, it is common for unexpected things to happen – unexpected encounters with all sorts of different types of people. I have had it suggested to me that people might talk to me in a particular way because of my own particular demeanour – an older person who somehow looks as though they might not judge or interpret as others might. This observation though needs to be set against the fact that all of us have peculiarities on one sort or another.

The British teacher's annoyance also resonates with the Orientalist grand narrative, where 'we Westerners value our privacy' and 'those Chinese do not because of their collectivism', which is the basis of my initial shock described in Chapter 3.

The multiple effect of 'the West'

It is though one thing for people 'from the West' to feel threatened by the imagined collectivism of the East and for people to be attacked or in other ways affected by the West whether abroad or at home. An example of this is what Mina[1] has to say when interviewed by Sara Amadasi. She is a newly arrived so-labelled 'international' student in a British university who identifies as not Western. She tells us about things that attack her cultural exclusivity in the street:

> 'We cannot adapt, we cannot accept them … we don't have such things in our culture. … for example, a boyfriend and girlfriend hugging themselves in the street … we cannot accept it … we cannot do it.'
>
> (2017: 262, citing interview)

She then, when asked about diversity, does provide a more complex picture of something less culturally exclusive:

> 'The world is changing and … and for example I am a religious person … but doesn't mean the other is a very religious person like me … They are atheist in fact … but not to the extent … [that] I face it here.'
>
> (263–264, citing interview)

However, as she continues to speak about her own society, 'Western cultures' become a problematic and invasive Other. The complex nature of this Western Other is evident in how she associates it with Indian cinema – where the West is constructed as a global discoursal force that threatens the local:

> 'Imitation of the Western cultures especially through films and cinema. … and Facebook for example or social networks … and internet websites. … Decades ago … the bride cannot see her

---

1 In the original paper she is referred to as S1. I am naming her with this pseudonym for ease of reading.

husband until the day they marry him ... But nowadays, due to many developments, technological developments ... Indian films are dominated ... I have my niece, she's imitating the Indians in every single thing she wears ... then she went out with her boyfriend trying to imitate that love story.'

(2017: 264–265, citing interview)

Whether she thinks that Indian cinema has itself become a voice of the West or she is expanding her conceptualisation of what the West might actually be, Mina is talking about a power of influence that pervades everywhere.

I have spent time on this example because it makes me think again about what was happening to me in the shop in Tehran and its implication for my broader 'Western' presence. It might not just have been a matter of working out the arbitrary body language of fitting in. There might also have been at least a tinge of the Westerner being put in their place. The following shop setting of a different kind also helps me to make sense.

Western as Centre thinking everywhere

Mina's location of Western corruptive influence in Indian cinema takes the notion of the West away from a geographical area and into a broader idea of the Centre – the entity that attempts to define who we are from a position of power, as discussed in Chapter 1. This to me resonates with the following incident that took place perhaps a year after my arrival with Maya, a colleague at the British Council who, significantly, I had heard identify as 'not Western':

I was in a grocery shop with Maya. Just in front of us, being served, was who we presumed to be an Iranian woman perhaps in her mid-1930s. We were both watching her and taking note of her appearance. After she had turned and left the shop, Maya commented that there was 'so much adulterated beauty in Iran'. My understanding of what she meant was that the woman had a beauty that had been spoilt by the way in which she dressed and wore make-up. Maya was five to ten years older than me and, in my view, a more experienced professional and world traveller. She had been in Iran for perhaps a year longer than me; and I considered her to a degree as a mentor. I colluded with her opinion of the woman's appearance.

This collusion was partly because there was a strong narrative among my other newcomer colleagues that Iranian society lacked taste in its preference for exaggeration in styles from clothing to advertising images, shop decoration and home and office furniture. While I bought into this narrative, I was at the same time aware of some ambivalence due to my alternative experience of how my Iranian reference group and their milieu explicitly professed high standards regarding style and class.

My collusion with Maya's negative cultural evaluation, despite the complex modernity and hybridity I was experiencing elsewhere, was seductively Orientalist, the underlying Centre narrative being that 'people outside the West do not have the individualist sophistication to manage their newly arrived modernity'. That 'not Western' Maya should subscribe to this Centre discourse is perhaps surprising – especially when she was also someone who claimed integration into Iranian society by virtue of the 'Iranian friends' of whom she often spoke.

I mention this incident because it represents a number of times when other people there could have sensed what was going on in the minds of the newcomer customers. It did not occur to me that 'not Western' Maya could be associated with 'Western' judgement until I recalled Mina referring to Indian cinema as Western. This is not however surprising if one considers that Orientalism as a Centre grand narrative, while being a Western invention with which to imagine the East and the South, has no boundaries regarding who can be invaded by it. I say 'invaded' because I do not think that many of us not so much choose but are seduced by grand narratives – attracted by stories that respond to all sorts of circumstances that surround us. What this means is that the Centre, Western, Orientalist grand narrative was very much evident, and indeed appropriated in many aspects of how different types of people, including Iranians who identified with particular positionalities, presented themselves and their views.

It needs to be remembered that the Orientalist grand narrative is a development of a more common narrative about a deficient Other. Kubota (2001) makes the point very well that essentialist stereotypes of East Asian students in English classes in the United States are very similar to those of underperforming mainstream American students who are also characterised as lacking critical thinking and autonomy. It is therefore quite possible that some of my colleague Maya's Iranian friends might themselves have fed her with narratives of deficiency among people that they considered not as able as them to acquire a sophistication of style and taste that they themselves associated with perhaps an imagined Western élite with whom they liked to position *themselves* – and perhaps with which she also associated herself.

The ubiquity of positioning around Centre power

I need however to try and pin this down. What seems to be happening is perhaps something like this: Centre thinking is by its nature something that becomes ubiquitous as either a force through which we look or one that we resist. The term 'Orientalist' is not so well known as an association with the Centre. 'Western' however is very well-known in its association with personal freedoms, whether these be considered desirable or corruptive. The following statements about culture can therefore be encountered among people who would not identify themselves as 'Western', even in the same person. They represent what I have heard people say in a number of settings:

- 'Western ideas about disregard for tradition in Indian films are corrupting our young people.'
- 'Our government prevents any sort of advancement in which anything like Western society can develop.'
- 'People here claim that they have achieved Western ways of life; but they are just imitating.'
- 'We don't need the West to tell us how to be modern.'

The implication of the range of statements like this is that, whoever talks about the West for whatever reason, it represents a locus of Centre power around which people position themselves with a considerable degree of either tacit or explicit anxiety. While the first and last statements indicate clear resistance, the other two, when spoken by the same person, indicate the ambivalence between the lines of this resistance. It is on this basis that I imagine an ambivalence regarding my frequent presence in a local shop that might get in the way of treating and serving me like the other customers. Also, again, what was different about the shared taxis was that they were never the same driver or group of other passengers. An interesting analysis of the complexities of the popular and state voicing of subalternity in Iran in more recent times can be found in Holliday (2016d). Regardless of who speaks the Orientalist grand narrative, for whatever purpose, and even unconsciously, it represents a deeply judgemental set of beliefs that, from a position of global authority, reduce others to a racist stereotype.

This complexity is also a further sign of the hybridity that is the major basis of my ability to participate – that all of us are multiple things, taking part in multiple discourses of culture for different reasons at different times. There is therefore a hybrid response to the power of Western judgement of which I am also a part.

A subtle Western invasion of space

Further evidence of the ubiquity of the effect of the West can be seen in the following description of Mahnaz's experience of what might seem on the surface to be a very innocent outing with British people. For clear or unclear reasons it brings her a feeling of being invaded:

> Mahnaz told me that she'd been out with a British family – two adults and two young children. They'd taken her in their car out of town to a village resort in the mountains. She was surprised at what the family talked about. When I asked her what she meant, she said it was what they noticed at the side of the road and in the scenery as they passed, what they chose to say about it, how they discussed it, what they generally found interesting, and the number of times that they pointed things out to each other. Mahnaz said that these were things that Iranians would not think worthy of comment.
>
> She did seem a bit annoyed, as though it was an assault on her personal space. She then went on to say that she found it annoying that British people seemed to need to explain, ask questions and apologise about things that just didn't need it – almost as though they lacked the intelligence to understand quietly. The most unimportant things had to be pulled out and pulled apart.

One, and I stress, superficial, reading of this is the traditional, essentialist picture of large culture difference which would maintain that Iranian and British 'cultures' have different communication modes. An Orientalist interpretation would take this further to assume that the British family is being more critical and analytical in individualist discussion of the world around them and that the more collectivist Iranian 'culture' does not allow the expression of individualist viewpoints and personal opinion about the world. This reading is perhaps what is annoying Mahnaz, though she may not be aware of its particular politics, in that she is feeling victim to Western judgement. Why else would she be annoyed that different people talk about different types of things?

Certainly, Mahnaz shows no evidence of this proposed cultural inability in the way that she tells me about what happened. Instead, her tone is more about how limited the family seems to be in what they chose to look at and how they seemed to waste their time stating the obvious. We do not though know how she came over to the British family at the time. She may well have been driven to silence by what she may have felt to be an invasion. Neither do we know whether or not any of the British people in the car indicated any sense of 'Western superiority'. It could be unlikely that they did – in the same way as I had little awareness of the presence of Westernness until Bahman told me how he compared himself to me.

A perhaps more worrying possible interpretation is that Mahnaz is annoyed because she is feeling marginalised because she also perceives that she is 'not performing' according to what she thinks might be the Western ideal that she wishes to claim but cannot.

Another, simpler, possibility is that the newcomer family is simply noticing and looking around at everything because it is unfamiliar, in the same way as the newcomers walking in the streets in Chapter 4 – which is another reason for Mahnaz to be annoyed, as were the taxi passengers. A small culture reading might be that whenever one spends time with a different sort of group than one is used to, whether they be fine-art connoisseurs or a particular family, one might find that they notice and talk about things in an esoteric manner as they employ discourses that are specific to their interests and orientations. This will also happen when one travels, not necessarily to distant lands, but anywhere that changes one's preoccupations – new employment or relationships. I was noticing different sorts of things while in Iran compared to when I lived in Britain – and noticed things when I returned to Britain that I had not before, as I did when I returned to the village where I lived as a child and also to my parents' home.

There is an interesting point here about language. When I spent time with an Iranian family group while they were sitting and socialising, I felt excluded because my Farsi was not sufficient to join in the conversation and to get the finer detail of what they were talking about. I spent time noticing all the non-verbal aspects of communication and often developed theories about what was going on. Some of which would certainly have been coloured by the Orientalist grand narrative. When I spent time with my extended family in Britain while they were sitting and socialising, I also felt excluded. I understood every word and the histories that went with it, but was not able to join in because I had outgrown what they were interested in and found it all the more annoying *because* I understood every word. I also theorised about what was going on in a way that was partly influenced by prejudices of social class.

Mahnaz's sense of being invaded is nevertheless real; and whether or not she herself might sense a 'Western' issue, in one way or another, is I think somewhere between the lines of her 'British' car journey.

Blatant imperialism

Very much not between-the-lines is the incident involving American soldiers in a taxi that I will look at next. It is beyond the scope of this book to look at the global politics regarding Iran and the West at the time that I was there, leading up to the 1979 revolution that expelled the large majority of Western foreigners. Suffice it to say that underpinning the nuances of relations with the concept of the West was a very obvious US military presence. I never encountered any explicit conflict between the different types of people in the taxi until I witnessed the following:

> In the back of the taxi were two uniformed American soldiers. I sat in the front seat next to the driver. I didn't know how much of what they were saying the driver could understand. They were complaining to each other in quite loud voices about the way they were swindled by a waiter in a restaurant. I was quite pleased that they didn't seem to recognise me as another Western newcomer. At least they didn't acknowledge this. Perhaps they thought that it was just part of the normal scene and therefore didn't make any particular acknowledgement of my presence. Why should they? They seemed to me to be unaware of their surroundings. Iranians, to me, had loud voices. It wasn't therefore the loudness of their voices that jarred, but their whole manner of somehow taking over the whole space as though they automatically owned it as though their own image of 'civilisation' was very explicitly the only norm.

It was perhaps because of the vibrancy of the bustling city that I had not noticed this sort of explicit conflict before. It would be wrong to jump to the blanket conclusion that these two 'behaving badly' soldiers were characteristic of American military personnel in Iran. I had heard some young Iranians speak of American soldiers as romantic figures from the fabled country that every younger person I met seemed to want to go to. Simin told me that she and her friends wrote secret notes to American soldiers to practise their English when she was in secondary school. This admiration did not in itself seem strange to me at a time when American television programmes were still dominant in Britain and people in my family swooned at the sight of American cars, and cowboys were still our heroes with the allure of the 'wide-open spaces' of the 'wild' West. I was at that time myself conscious of an ambivalent relationship. My grandmother, who was by no means widely read, was an avid reader of Zane Grey Western novels (e.g. 1912).

It was however the 'explicit' nature of the soldiers' enacted superiority that got to me. Perhaps it also made me uncomfortably recognise my own deep feeling of cultural superiority, which surfaced more unconsciously in the shop with my colleague Maya. At the same time, it also occurred very strongly to me at the time that the two soldiers had violated the small culture (though I did not know the term) equilibrium of taxi life that I had experienced directly up until that point. It was not just creating blocks instead of seeking threads, but what seemed to be a blatant disregard for what was going on around them.

Through the eyes of others

This ambivalent sensitivity to Centre Western presence and attitudes of superiority was also evident in my experience, looking out from shared taxis, of how my Iranian co-travellers might have viewed Western newcomers they saw in the streets:

> Once I seemed to have acquired more successful alignment with objects and people, I began to notice, as I was travelling by taxi, new 'foreigners' walking in the street. They were recognisable from the way in which they explicitly looked at everything as they walked – like frightened animals on the lookout for predators and storms, or people beleaguered by unexpected missiles from unknown directions – or just explicitly looking at almost everything as strange. I also recall other passengers in the taxi noticing this, sometimes with varying degrees of annoyance, and sometimes laughing at them.
>
> There was also a matter of attitude there sometimes, when they wore exaggerated versions of exotic local clothing. Iranian city dwellers and the middle classes had, half a century before, on their own terms and in a highly discerning manner, claimed ownership of what might previously have been considered 'Western' styles of clothing. Even the religious head or body covering of those women who chose it was most often over so-labelled Western styles. Therefore, Western newcomers wearing what they thought was 'indigenous' clothing' (e.g. turbans, felt hats, loose tunics, sashes

and woven cotton shoes) could be interpreted as insulting or even exoticising.

Here therefore I felt that I was beginning to see people like myself when I first arrived through 'local' eyes. Once again, the politics of looking was evident. While explicit looking seemed a cultural norm, as discussed in the interview with Sara in Chapter 4, it also depended on what was being looked at and for what purpose. The way that my colleague Maya in the shop appeared to be looking might be interpreted as Centre evaluation of a consequentially marginalised Other. The improper and exoticising reference by newcomer foreigners to traditional clothing denied modernity; and there was implied suspicion about stealing and cheating. Regarding the latter, I had of course heard Iranians complaining about how people in the bazar might cheat you; but it was very different when this came from a Centre Western foreigner.

It is important to make the point of caution again and again, that this is not to say that there are not taxi drivers and bazar traders in Iran who do not cheat and worse. However, my overall point is that this is behaviour one will find in all societies and not the result of collectivist, indolent cultural values that preclude personal responsibility and quite a different thing to the easy accusations that came from some 'foreign' friends and colleagues, always to complain and accuse taxi drivers and other traders of trying to swindle and cheat. That this easy accusing might become a self-fulfilling prophecy might indeed have something to do with, but not excused by, tensions set up by annoying 'foreigner' behaviour. This would be mirrored by the tensions, especially perhaps in pre-revolutionary Iranian society, concerning annoyance from more traditional quarters with apparently insensitive displays of what were considered inappropriately revealing Western dress styles among some Iranian women.

The advantage of gender

This reference to the experience of women did relate to the advantage that I had as a male rather than a female Western newcomer. I did become aware of this soon after arriving in Iran, when I compared my experiences with those of several Western women newcomer friends. They had a harder time than I did if they were living with Iranian families. There was certainly a degree of patriarchy that automatically placed a male newcomer in a position of status. At the same time, I heard accounts from Iranian as well as Western women about sexual abuse on the street and in taxis both from other passengers and taxi drivers. I know of a particular Iranian woman who received racist comments that were aimed at her darker skin colour. This was how-ever a highly complex issue that could not be explained in any way by the common collectivist stereotype. While I in no way wish to di-minish the seriousness of patriarchal forces and difficulties that many women had, I do feel that we need to be very cautious of an essentialist rumour among Western teachers – that 'non-Western cultures have no respect for women teachers' when one can argue that patriarchy is everywhere, sometimes less visible, but equally destructive.

The following event serves to show how the reality could be very subtly, but very importantly different to the expected:

> Mahnaz told me that she'd been walking in an uptown shopping street with her British husband. The street was not crowded, but there were other people also walking along nearby, promenading or perhaps on their way to the cinema. It was still daylight. She said that they were being careful not to hold hands or show other forms of physical affection that weren't allowed in public places.
>
> A car with several men inside drove slowly along the road next to them. She noticed that the men were watching them. The car then drove a little ahead, stopped, and one of the men got out and walked towards them. He stopped and addressed Mahnaz di-rectly and politely. He asked her if she was being bothered by this 'foreigner' and if she needed any assistance. He also apologised if he was being inappropriately intrusive, and explained that they had been watching them for some time trying to work out whether or not it was necessary or appropriate to offer assistance. When Mahnaz explained, also politely and directly that she wasn't in danger, and also thanked him for his concern, the man immedi-ately got back in the car, which promptly drove off.

This is very close to the common Orientalist expectation of the East-ern woman under collectivist patriarchal scrutiny because she is asso-ciating individualistically with a so-framed morally corrupt Western foreigner. Such a construction might include the belief that that the woman would be punished or outcast. However, Mahnaz emphasised that this was not at all what was going on. While it was clear that the man approached her because she was with a foreigner, she framed it differently to the expected reasons – as his genuine concern for her safety:

> Mahnaz said that this reminded her of another event when she was walking in the street from one shop to another, also with her

husband, and a man approached her to say that he'd been following her for a short while because he noticed that her bag was open
and was concerned that someone might steal her wallet that was
visible within it.

She said said that there was no doubt that in each case that the
man who 'came to her assistance' was absolutely honourable, sincere, cautious and genuinely caring in his intentions. She also said
that it was not uncommon for Iranian people to look out for each
other in public places.

We have no idea what was going on in the minds of the people in the
car, of the men who approached Mahnaz, or the other people in the
street who would undoubtedly be looking on. If we were in a position
to interview each of the men who approached her, they may well claim
collectivist culture principles. If they did, we would not know what
deeper politics of positioning might be going on that led them to make
essentialist statements about culture, or whether grand narratives
were being blindly followed or being played with. In the case of the
American soldier in the taxi, we have no idea what might be going on
in his mind either. He might have been recovering from a trauma and
have been acting out of character. It was not uncommon to see Iranians in public places displaying aggressive anger brought on by the life
pressures that they were facing in a society that was by no means at
peace with itself because of ongoing political pressures.

If such events were witnessed in the present, to get to the bottom of
what was going on would require far more than interviews. Relevant
here is Geertz's often-cited account of how it is necessary to research
what is going on between the onlookers to find out that a boy is wink-
ing to parody another boy who is twitching (1993: 6). The plea for thick
description in his account implies that we need to look far wider than
particular statements. None of the examples that I am finding in this
book are designed to 'prove' that Iran 'is not a collectivist culture'.
They are instead building a picture of interconnected instances – a
thick description – to say that there is no reason to believe that Iranian
society is any more collectivist than anywhere else other than being
driven by a racist Orientalist grand narrative.

Social norms plus the politics of how we are received

It needs to be noted that Mahnaz in the above accounts was with her
husband. There would be no way that the people in the street would
know this. Even in 'Western countries' where shows of physical

affection are common, unless we know people, we cannot tell what their relationships are – spouse, partner, boyfriend girlfriend, just very good friends, or so on. It was however important that they were not holding hands and social norms for the streets of Tehran were being observed. I say Tehran because in rural areas it would be different again. These are practices that simply need to be learned along with using certain implements to eat certain food, and all the sorts of practices described in Chapter 3. These are things that can be learned or resisted wherever they are found, beginning with the family next door. That I never could do group-sleeping during siesta time set me apart as having a particular personality rather than as being 'British'. If I did not like some Iranian food because it was too dry, was this no different to Bahram being well known for not liking the common Iranian ingredient of onions?

Whether or not, like Mina, earlier in the chapter, one gets annoyed or exaggerates, there is also diversity and huge change. This is part of the creative tapestry that makes up cultural life and stretches beyond borders. This is exemplified in the account in (Holliday 2019: 169–173) in which Safa learns about how and where she can practise her agency to effect cultural innovation at home and abroad. There is however a need for politeness to go with the norms of what is acceptable. Indeed, it was partly on this basis that I felt that the two American soldiers in the taxi, above, were simply disregarding what was going on around them in the pursuit of their own agendas prejudices. This is not much different to how a researcher needs to learn how to blend sufficiently to gain acceptance from the people they want to watch or talk to in social settings. This is part of the data that we all need to consider when positioning or repositioning ourselves when confronted by the intercultural.

The examples so far in this chapter do however indicate that there *is* a major difference, not in whether people are culturally individualist or collectivist, but in the inequality of how they are regarded. Faultlines created by how Centre perceptions define the rest of the world bring about circumstances where in different ways among different people there is a large or small politics of *those who receive prejudice and those who give it out* – always being defined or defining. This Centre does not have to be Western or Orientalist. It just so happens that in the scenarios that I am looking at, the particular content of defining or being defined is often prevalent, especially with regard to a European sojourner in a place that has been hugely mythologised in European narratives, and where there is a confusion between modernity versus tradition and being Western or not. Thinking again about the

American soldiers in the taxi, who, as I have already said, may not be like other American soldiers, whether Western or not, we all I think know about people from all walks of life who are sufficiently arrogant or ignorant to only follow their own agendas, or those of their group, in blatant disregard for anyone around them.

Being my English self

The overall implication of the analysis so far in this chapter seems to be that while I had an advantage because of my undoubted Western status, not just in how I was seen by others, but in the automatic confidence that it brought. While I might have had life made difficult for me because of the complex ambivalence towards the West and the Centre gaze that it represented, I was of the people *who give out prejudice rather than receive it.* Hence, the rationale for this book – to get to the bottom of the nature of this Orientalist prejudice and how to put it aside.

However, it also becomes clear that making it easier for me to be accepted was by no means in imitation of what could only be a prejudiced and exoticised, stereotypical, essentialist, and indeed Orientalist image of 'Iranian life and culture'. I should not be associated with those Western foreigners who were looked upon with humour and anger. To be taken seriously by my fellow taxi passengers, I needed to be my English self in everything that I did and thought. This was in how I spoke Farsi, which relates to the hybrid nature of language and its relationship with culture.

This was to do with showing appreciation to the people I engaged with that we all equally had the ability to see the richness of hybridity of both modernity and tradition in each other to find genuine threads with who we all were. This was therefore a powerful lesson in sincerity and cultural belief – which I have defined elsewhere as belief 'that the cultural background of *any* person is rich and resourceful to the extent that it can be engaged with, learned from and indeed expanded into' (Holliday 2019: 157).

Are taxis in Tehran too accessible?

Something else that readers might think is that it was easier for me to claim so much connection with taxis in Tehran because there were so many elements of modernity that I could recognise and feel comfortable with. Perhaps a different sort of image comes from this account by Sara Amadasi of her experience of travelling by a form of crowded public transport when she was a student researcher in Senegal at the age of 27 in 2009. Here she describes what she observed regarding a form of public transport in Senegal:

> Car-rapides are vans with a rear opening, used for passenger transport. Inside there are seats, arranged to fill all the space possible and therefore to contain as many people as possible.
>
> (Amadasi 2010: 115)

An easy take on this, based on the Orientalist prejudice, might be that the car-rapide is therefore a chaotic, tightly crowded place with very little possibility of personal space or safety. But what she recalls as the description continues is however very different – an unexpected order and respect for individuals:

> In 2009, on car-rapides, generally worked two or three people, all males. While one is driving, the others – the so-called 'car-rapide apprentices' – stay behind. They are the ones who do the hardest work because, in order not to occupy a place inside the van, they cling to the rear and outside of the vehicle. In this way they can warn the driver when to stop and when to start again by tapping with one hand – possibly with a large ring – on the side of the van. It is also up to them to collect the money, which happens in a rather unusual way in the eyes of a toubab[2]: the first in line, being the furthest away from the 'controller', will let their money reach the latter by passing it from hand to hand towards the bottom and saying, out loud, their destination. The same happens with the change, which will be sent to the passenger through the same method. Normally this practice seems to take place in total trust and transparency, so that, in two months and numerous trips in car-rapides, it has never happened to me to witness quarrels or disagreements caused by a wrong 'management' of the accounts, neither by the 'controller' nor by the passengers.
>
> The car-rapides apprentices therefore remain in this condition of 'suspension' in full city traffic, forced most of the time to jump on the already moving car-rapides. For all these reasons, the work of the car-rapides apprentice can be very difficult, dangerous, and there are many young people in the village who tell of their numerous fractures due to this occupation.
>
> (p. 115)

---

2 Toubab is a term used in Central- and West-Africa for European.

She learned about the unexpected, for, as she says, a European, passing fares from the back of the vehicle to the driver. Like me, she began to understand the order and the professionalism of the people who worked there, which, in turn, taught her to overcome the collectivist stereotype. She later told me though, that this seeing through her prejudice was not immediate and happened slowly during her stay of three months. It was one thing to understand quickly that what was happening inside the vehicle was not an indolent free-for-all. It was another to begin to recognise that, as with the passengers in the Tehran taxi, the people there were also always hybrid in that they represented the agentive diversity of Senegalese society. The bigger point, again and again, is why we should always begin with the collectivist stereotype as a prime assumption as soon as we venture outside the West. The burden of proof should not be against a stereotype that begins with a racist Orientalist grand narrative.

Applying the grammar

In this chapter the value of applying the grammar of culture is particularly salient in that being forced to think about its various domains enables me to see things that I had not previously. Therefore, in Figure 6 I begin to make more new sense of the discussion in this chapter.

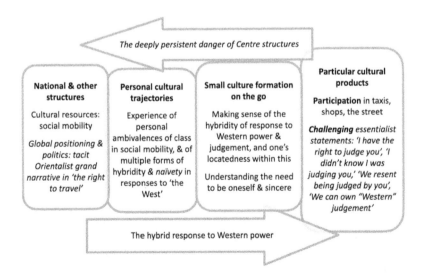

Figure 6 Grammar of culture (Western newcomers).

In the top arrow, it is very clear that Centre structures, which include the Western presence, are never going to go away. The same applies to gender, which is only briefly referred to but relates to the world-wide Centre institution of patriarchy. This is evident in the feeling of the 'right to travel' (bottom left), which is also an undeniable presence throughout the chapter.

However, the bottom arrow indicates an understanding about the nature of a hybrid response in observed Iranian society that mediates against the Centre, in this case, Western power. This is what is learned in small culture formation on the go (centre right), where sense is made of how Western judgement does not only come from so-labelled 'Western' people, and how I as the newcomer am located within this – hence my *participation* (right middle).

The personal cultural trajectory and cultural resources domains of the grammar force me to consider what I have brought from experience that enables me to make some sense of what is going on. Hence, I recall my own social mobility in my upbringing – being the first person in my family to get a university education and moving from what was then a very culturally different North to study and work in the South. Also, the other way round, I spent my childhood in a middle-class family in a largely working-class village and always felt an outsider. This mobility was not extreme, but enabled a sensitivity with which to appreciate hybrid responses to Centre forces.

Then, in the back-and-forth manner that I have focused on in this book, my trajectory led me to observe similar hybridity in reading response to the West in my experience of living and working in Syria and Egypt since leaving Iran, further compounded by a continued personal feeling of disjuncture between my lower middle-class upbringing and the élite middle-classness of my British Council employer. I was able to survive and find myself in this disjuncture through my and their hybridity. It is this that helped me to realise the value of being myself and sincere (middle right bottom).

It also helped me to see the hybrid nature of multiple and sometimes contradicting statements about culture (bottom right) that involved people claiming ownership of Western judgement. This appreciation of hybridity by no means diminishes the inequality and Othering created by the way in which Centre structures define everyone in a West-rest image. While hybridity allows for a degree of appropriation of Western judgement, there is also the deep resentment of being judged, which I sensed was deep within how I was sometimes also treated as a newcomer.

6 Stories, media, and histories

This chapter will look at how I continued to make sense of life in Iran through immersion in an almost totally different set of cultural references to those that travel across Europe. These comprise children's stories, myths and histories of nation, ancient literatures, poems, songs and music, theatre, fabrics, and motifs. However, as with spaces and the impact of being Western in the previous chapters, I will demonstrate that my emerging understanding of hybridity took me far from the expected difference between the imagined two large national or civilisational 'cultures' falsely created by the Orientalist grand narrative.

An immediate way in

I speak here from my memory of my own experience and not from an academic, scholarly perspective, when I recall that the obvious exceptions in the list of unfamiliar cultural references are fabrics and motifs. It is well known that Persian carpets have been very present and influential across the Western world; and the designs have become common everywhere.

I have a distinct childhood memory of a linoleum floor covering in my grandmother's bathroom having what I later discovered to be a Persian carpet design. Another childhood memory is of my other grandmother embroidering table cloths with the paisley motif which is derived from the Persian *boteh*. Much of this would also have come to Britain via India and the Moghul influence. I have already mentioned in Chapter 2 that I was familiar with the Iranian poet, Omar Khayyam; and I think that it was common knowledge that Iran had a long literary tradition.

The children's stories, myths, and histories of nation were unknown to me. In my experience, they largely derived from Islamic imageries

DOI: 10.4324/9781003039174-6

which I later found to be common across the Middle East, North Africa, and across to Pakistan in my sojourns and interactions with colleagues and students there, and pre-Islamic Persian imageries which I later found also travelled to a degree in the Middle East and the Indian sub-continent to the near extent of the Persian Empire and Moghul influence. They were however conceptually accessible because they had a form that resonated with the European imageries that I was used to. The 11th-century epic poem that depicted the myth of nation, the *Shahnameh*, the book of kings, to me, fell into the same grand trope as the 11th century Anglo-Saxon *Beowulf*. Many of the stories had to me the familiar form of heroes, unrequited love, mistaken identity, rescue, monsters, battles, chivalry, and so on. My recognition of this in itself helped to forge a major thread that immediately began to dissolve large culture national or civilisational essentialist boundaries. While the difference of cultural reference was very clearly there, I began to see quickly that these references, which populated everyday language, worked in a very similar way to how the equivalent references worked in my own upbringing. I feel that this was therefore instead a healthy and non-essentialist conversation between civilisations with a huge recognition of mutual hybrid underpinnings.

Unexpected threads across and between

Hence, while I did not at that time have the technical language to explain this, I was witnessing an underlying universal cultural process that was enabling me to get threads from unexpected directions, not only from my prior intercultural experience but across experiences I was beginning to have in Iran.

This is reflected in this memory of making sense of a play despite lack of language because of what I was also getting from the radio and a broader atmosphere of reference:

> I was taken to the theatre by Iranian friends to see an avant garde play. While my Farsi was by now fairly good on a one-to-one conversational basis, I could hardly understand anything of the detail of what was being said by the actors. However, when, afterwards, I told my friends what I thought was going on in the play, they were astonished how much of its overall message and force I had understood. Indeed, they thought that I had caught the ideological message of the performance. In fact, throughout the performance, I was totally engaged. It was the imagery, the intonation and the posturing that I was able to follow in what seemed to me a familiar trope.

It was however familiar in a convoluted way. I remember thinking during the performance that there were connections with what I had gleaned about the verbal force of the *Shahnameh*, the Persian myth of nation, and the sounds that I had heard in recitations of poetry on the radio, put together with how I was beginning to understand that these were somehow employed in topical political opposition, that this was taking me into what was going on on the stage.

A particular thread that I remember was with seeing satirical comedy on television that in turn connected with similar media at home:

With Iranian friends at home, we often watched the popular satirical television show, *Dooset daram dooset daram*, I love you I love you, in which I could see a use of intonation and posturing which, though very different detail, to what had been emerging on television in Britain, had an overall form that I could understand. The Farsi was relatively accessible because of the strong locatedness in exaggerations of everyday scenarios that I had also witnessed while out and about in the city.

The greater accessibility of language here connected with café storytelling, that connected back with the play:

Sitting in a downtown café and witnessing the traditional storyteller reciting scenes from the *Shahnameh*. It was powerfully visual. He stood in front of a large hand-painted picture of a gory scene in which the hero was slicing in half his enemy. The style of the picture, while not the same, somehow resonated with those which I had seen on street and cinema posters. Especially the latter carried some of the hyperbole about stereotyped good and evil that was also very evident in the story teller's performance. I was now also getting used to, and indeed perhaps clumsily participating in, the way in which the audience sat and occupied their space in what I was also beginning to understand to be a mixing of traditional and modern styles and aspirations. The way in which the storyteller stood, moved and used intonation to communicate powerful and heroic gestures was what I had also seen, though I very different ways, in the posturing of the actors in the play and the satirical comedians on television.

The final sentences, explaining the 'the mixing of traditional and modern styles and aspirations' across the extreme modernity in the intellectual underpinning of the avant garde play, the modernity of the satire, both taking forms from the *Shahnameh* and also found in the café story that was steeped in tradition was drawing my attention to the nature of complex threads in any society. This was also the hybridity that was evident in the taxis in Chapter 4, which were threads within the society that I was beginning to see and helping me to make sense.

Perhaps as small validation of this interconnecting between different forms within and across multiple cultural scenarios, my informant, Irene, tells me the following (based on email and interview):

> She was shown a video clip of Kabuki theatre in her contemporary Japanese society class while studying in Japan. While she believed that she already had a very rich linguistic and cultural background, she did not understand anything, not even the plot, not even an ounce of words. The figures moved in front of her eyes without any apparent sense. She later found it on YouTube with subtitles. She first watched without the subtitles, this time focusing only on the facial expressions. Surprisingly, she felt she already knew what expression would come next. Once she put on the subtitles, she had the strong emotion of being able to connect the sounds to the movements in a sort of part-by-part reconstruction of what she was seeing.
>
> When I asked her what she brought from her Italian upbringing that helped her to gain this understanding, after some thought she said that it was her childhood experience of the marionette puppet shows.

Learning about my own society

What I was noticing explicitly in the strangeness of Iran was therefore also educating me more in the sociology of my upbringing. Indeed, this was externalising the nature of connections that take place throughout our lives but which we might not be aware of until we find ourselves in a more explicitly strange environment. Therefore, while I might have thought, between the cinema, the television, and the café, that I was searching for meanings in this way for the first time, I had in fact done it many times before. An example of this might surely have been going to concerts in Leeds Town Hall in my late teens, attending a public lecture in London by Karl Popper in my early 1920s, watching *The brains trust*, a television quiz programme with famous philosophers, in my mid teens, and listening to my school headmaster addressing the morning school assembly in my early teens. In each of these, there was much that I did not understand at the time both in terms of language and the politics and positioning of the event. However, there were rhythms and demeanours in common that helped me to build aspects of understanding that enabled me to begin to understand what was going on. In the cases of the concert and the lecture, I had learned enough of these to be able to find them and work out how to attend when no one in my family had ever done such things before.

It may well also be that I was finding in Iran the things that resonated, albeit unconsciously, with my own upbringing – with the intellectual development that I was bringing with me. I remember that the Iranian avant garde novel that I read, translated into English, was Sadegh Hedayat's *Bouf-e kour*, The blind owl (1937/1958). This was a widely translated classic that reminded me of the work that I had recently read of Franz Kafka, which was popular with my peers.

Finding these threads was also tapping into the underlying politics of Iran at the time, which is beyond the scope of this book but is to do, as in many other places, with a society searching for its identity through complex threads of history. A discussion of how themes from the *Shahnameh* continue to influence the identities of Iranian youth 40 years later can be found in Honarbin-Holliday (2013).

More cosmopolitan than me

There was also what I might have felt to be a further twist in my discovery of something similar to Kafka in Iranian literature. The following recollection exemplifies this:

> Simin had some of the same Russian, French and Ancient Greek classics on her book shelves as I had – Tolstoy, Chekov, Flaubert, Plato and others. Whereas mine were translated into English, hers were translated into Farsi. There was also European classical music in their home – Beethoven, Mozart, Schubert and so on. These of course needed no translation. But there was also something that I could think of no equivalent in my home. There were music albums of the British psychedelic progressive folk band, *The incredible string band* and the American rock musical, *Hair*. These were what her elder sister had brought back from a recent stay in Britain as an engineering student. What struck me was that this taste in music represented a marginal taste and knowledge that I had previously associated with a particular group of British youth. Another book on the shelf was *Present day English for*

foreign students in which were descriptions of the British families going about their daily business to provide examples of how English was used. These artefacts of culture stood alongside a library of Persian literature and classical and traditional Iranian music.

While these were things that I noticed in one person's home, I didn't meet anyone in Iran for whom it would seem that possessing 'foreign' cultural artefacts of one type or another should not be normal.

A major question regarding this description is why it should be considered worthy of note. My experience with Iranian people in Britain before travelling to Iran had already pulled me away from the easy prejudice that they should only like Iranian literature and music. Nevertheless, even though I had encountered Iranian people in Britain who were living, studying, and working there as though it was a normal aspect of their lives, I had not expected that there would be quite such a cosmopolitan viewpoint. While I found so much in this new Iranian world, while increasingly accessible, something that I had to work at to embrace, they seemed to find it a natural thing to do to embrace the whole world. In this sense, I was being taught a lesson in how to be cosmopolitan. There was also nothing new about the reference to Russian novels. In Kamali's novel, *The stationery shop of Tehran*, in 1953, another Iranian woman student reads 'all the translations of Russian novels' available in a city that is also 'blossoming with publishing, cinema, theatre, literature, and art' (2019: 79).

It is significant, I think, that it was here in an Iranian home that I was first introduced to *The incredible string band*. It was a vinyl record, and it was while in Iran that I bought my first audio cassette player and music to play on it. That Simin's sister was an engineer was also instrumental in my getting rid of the stereotype that I had had at that time that 'engineers' did not know about art and culture.

The soap opera and threads of family and class

While the experience at the theatre and its associations connected back and forth to the details of everyday life, there was also a television drama that was more obviously to do with the everyday:

During my first year in Iran I regularly watched the popular soap opera, *Talkh o shirin*,[1] bitter and sweet. My attention was drawn

---

1 Details of the series can be found at https://www.imdb.com/title/tt2318065/fullcredits/?ref_=tt_ov_st_sm.

by the interaction between two well-off middle class families, who I remember to be connected through a marriage. There was a tension because one family considered itself of a higher class than the other. This was marked by the 'higher class' family making fun of the 'lower class' because they made an ostentatious show of their expensive Mercedes family car and not wearing casual house clothes when relaxing with close friends and family at home.

This was particularly resonant with me because I saw a similar tension in family life in Britain. My own socially mobile family to me seemed more concerned with conspicuous consumption than those of more established middle class and indeed working-class peers, including that of my father's skilled working-class parents, as described for example in Hughes (2014). This also relates to my discussion of class, family, and the search for alternative living in Chapter 3. In the chapter, I was also able to understand most of what was being said in *Talkh o shirin* because the speech was slow and dramatic. I was also conscious of links in this dramatic form with the café storytelling, and then back to the *Shahnameh* referred to above.

This sort of resonance is illustrated in the following extract from Doshi's novel in which Indian Babo describes a scene from a Welsh family in the 1960s:

> It reminded Babo strangely of one of [his father] Prem Kumar's Sunday card-playing sessions. ... There was something very similar here, except in this Welsh-chintz version of the sideboard was heaving with devilled eggs instead of dhoklas. And instead of the sizeable paunches and behinds that middle-aged Gujjus succumbed to, these men and women were powerfully stocky, more uniform in their roundness. But there was the same parochial pride and failings on display. The same aunts berating an unmarried girl to hurry up and get on with it. The same know-all uncle complaining that a son was spending money like a man with no arms.
>
> (2010: 104–105)[2]

Indeed, the novel 'dances its people across barriers of race and nation' (Davies 2011). I have since found these resonances in a number of postcolonial novels where there is a recognisable ordinariness of everyday life despite religious and political distance and conflict. An example is

---

2 Further discussion of this extract can be found in Holliday (2019: 28).

with growing up as a teenager in the provincial town of Homs in Syria despite the backdrop of looming civil war (Nour 2020).

The danger of replacing one Othering with another – blocking threads and threading blocks

One might however critique both the Doshi extract and the soap opera as dealing only in dramatic stereotypes, and that basing my understanding of Iranian society on such imageries was replacing Orientalist for a simplistic Othering of class and gender. Davies's review of Doshi does make the point that 'the characters are simplified and idealised (especially the Welsh)'.

This is a serious concern. The danger of threads that in effect bring with them essentialist blocks, or *blocking threads*, is expressed by two characters in my book with Sara Amadasi. Kati and Eli find an intercultural thread that, in both 'their cultures', 'nobody really cares about public places and about keeping them clean and tidy – not like Western countries where everything seems to work'. They then realise that they are falling into the trap of colluding with the Western construction of them as culturally inferior. On realising this, they note that 'even in this "Western" country ..., you see rubbish lying around everywhere' (Holliday & Amadasi 2020: 56–57).

This lack of care with threads can also lead to a more sinister trap of threading blocks,[3] where there are ancient prejudices to do with race and gender that we can also share with people from different cultural backgrounds. This can be seen in the continuing conversation between Eli and Kati, where Kati notices Eli attempting to draw threads with her own experience by 'comparing people that she didn't like with a particular class or people from a particular region, and certainly sometimes sounding quite homophobic' (Holliday & Amadasi 2020: 60). It is also the case that soap operas can unconsciously perpetuate archetypal narratives of nation which can sometimes invoke conveniently forgotten racist pasts or presents (Marx Knoetze 2004, 2018).

However, to mediate this danger of Othering, I feel that I was, before travelling to Iran, to a degree aware of the sensationalist elements of soap operas per se, and, indeed, literary fiction. The issue is not whether our soap operas may contain stereotypical elements, but whether the cultural politics of such elements are appreciated by the

---

3 Further discussion of blocking threads and threading blocks can be found in Holliday (2020: 39–40).

people who watch or read them. The danger of an essentialist large culture approach is that it can falsely give the impression that one cannot transfer the sociological imagination one has with one's own society, that is, 'to understand the larger historical scene in terms of its meaning for the inner life and the external career of a variety of individuals' (Mills 1959/1970: 11), to a wider intercultural domain. We must not fall into the trap that Irving Goffman does when he says that:

> I did not mean to imply that the framework presented here is culture-free or applicable in the same areas of social life in non-Western societies as in our own. We lead an indoor life. We specialise in fixed settings, in keeping strangers out, and in giving the performer some privacy in which to prepare himself for the show. Once we begin a performance, we are inclined to finish it, and we are sensitive to jarring notes which may occur during it. If we are caught out in a misrepresentation we feel deeply humiliated. ... We must not overlook areas of life in other societies in which other rules are apparently followed.
>
> (1959/1990: 236–237)

This is an Orientalist trap in that it falsely implies that in non-Western cultures, people do *not* respect privacy, do *not* finish things and are not sensitive to 'jarring notes'.

The strong implication here is that, when I was able to find threads between stories, myths, and imageries that I found in Iran with those that I brought with me, I was also able to see the same principles that Goffman describes as 'presentation of self in everyday life' across both societies. Indeed, I should see common hybridities implicit in everyday life performance that Goffman, in the cited extract, somehow fails to have seen. The 'jarring notes' implicit in the stereotypical characterisations in the Iranian soap opera are also present in those to which I am more used. I thus begin to understand more about the hybridities in my own society.

Extending my critical knowledge of discourse and politics

This therefore means that when I was watching *Talkh o shirin*, I was being as critical of the implicit stereotypes as I was when watching soap operas in Britain, thus extending further my learning about my own society. I recognised it as part of the familiar soap opera genre *per se* – not as an Orientalist artefact. It did not represent a stereotype of 'Iranian culture', but instead the stereotypes that we *all* need to deal with regarding who we are everywhere. This did therefore serve to give me a strong sense of a wider perspective of my world rather than a limited perspective of someone else's. I did not have the same applied linguistics knowledge as I do now about the technical nature of discourses; but my sociology degree and an interest in the role of language in philosophy had made important contribution to my natural social and political awareness.

In the same way, it may well have been that it was in Iran that I began more deeply to understand the discourse features of political satire through watching the *Dooset daram dooset daram* television show referred to above. This may have been because I found the national politics in Iran more explicit and indeed more immediately dangerous than what I perceived to be the case in Britain. Despite the imperialist history referred to in Chapter 2, I had been relatively politically sheltered in Britain. Never having to have contemplated possible threat to my own family may indeed have contributed to my lack of awareness of the Orientalist grand narrative. The following quite frightening experience from my first week in Iran puts this into perspective:

> Hooshang took me aside to tell me that I needed to be very careful about who I spoke to and what I spoke about. He said that he'd heard that I travelled to Iran by train and thought that I had therefore probably spoken to fellow travellers that I didn't know. He also said that he'd heard me talking about Karl Marx and some of his books that I'd brought with me. He said that I needed to understand that if I spoke about politics or about people that I knew in public or with other people I didn't know well, it could have very serious consequences. He told me that he had had his passport confiscated by the police because he'd appeared on a photograph of a student demonstration against the Iranian government in Germany while he'd been studying there. He said that whole families could be arrested by the secret police and imprisoned.

My interest in Marx was to do with his sociology rather than his political Ideology. My immediate response was to associate the warning with the unconscious Orientalist imagery of summary execution referred to in Chapter 2. However, I quickly put this stereotype aside as I became aware of the sophisticated nature of the political fault lines of a modern state in which power was more explicitly visible and immediately life-threatening than in my own. The full force of the political satire in *Dooset daram dooset daram* became my model for the genre into the future. The intensely nuanced criticality is required to maintain intellectual opposition in the face of such power. That Iran was a place where summary execution could take place became clear when, near the end of my stay, a young man I had talked to about Omar Khayyam's poetry was shot by firing squad weeks later because of his role in the revolution. The unaccounted-for disappearance of students from classes at the British Council where I taught was not unknown.

This was a time when I was broadening my horizons. While I continued to have 'us'-'them' blocking interpretations, these were overtaken by new literatures, renewed understandings of familiar forms such as satire, soap, theatre, and music. That these happened to be mainly Iranian, and that I stopped reading European literature and listening to European classical music was to do with growing up in new circumstances and my developing hybridity. This was therefore a natural continuation of my personal cultural trajectory towards becoming a cosmopolitan citizen. Furthermore, this was not just because I was in Iran. It was also very largely because my life was changing and expanding anyway – being married, becoming a parent, having a new job, and having new interests.

DeCentred globalisation and claiming the world

Something that helps me to explain this finding and recognising elements of stories, histories, and media is that they represent discourses – specialist aspects of language and imagery that generate particular meaning – that can travel across cultural realities (Risager 2020: 118). This relates to the nature of linguaculture, which I will discuss further in Chapter 7. It is therefore discourses of theatre, soap opera, and satirical comedy, through finding them in Farsi as well as English.

Some readers might respond to this notion of transcendent discourses as being evidence of globalisation, where Iranian society has simply adopted Western forms. I prefer to see this as hybrid deCentred globalisation, where, in Stuart Hall's (1991) terms, the margins appropriate Centre ground in their own terms, as discussed in Chapter 1. This can be seen in the connections that I could see between these forms and traces from traditional linguistic forms in storytelling and the *Shahnameh*. That these are also multi-directional cultural flows can be seen in noticing of British appropriation of Iranian motifs referred to at the beginning of the chapter.

This image of Iranian people claiming the whole world while I felt a foreigner in theirs is well expressed in this extract of

Honarbin-Holliday's interview with an Iranian art student about how she claims Italian Renaissance art as part of her own heritage:

> 'When we studied the Renaissance, our tutor covered almost every single painter and every single brushstroke placed on a church wall in Italy during that period. ... You see I love art history, and it is ridiculous to separate West and East too much. If I am to be an artist, all of art history is my heritage. After all, we wouldn't tell a quantum physicist or a philosopher to skip the parts not related to their own geographical location, would we? Besides, I am a citizen of the globe, a member of the global village, I don't want to see myself as an artist who does not know what world art is all about.'
>
> (Honarbin-Holliday 2009: 77, citing interview text)

Because this interview took place many years later, after the 1979 revolution, one might have expected that the degree of isolation from the West would have been greater. Nevertheless, Honarbin-Holliday then comments:

> I am intrigued and inspired by this young woman. With just a few words she draws a picture of her world; this is a big world where her ideas, mind, and imagination can rise beyond geographical and cultural boundaries. She has determined her artistic identity to be complex and multi-dimensional.
>
> (p. 77)

While this also might be thought of as being an isolated event, Honarbin-Holliday takes this observation of claiming the world as a major theme for her book that applies to a diverse range of women of all ages in her study, including a germination already middle aged when I went to Iran in 1973. How Iranians position themselves in the world is also influenced by the presence of their significant global diaspora. While much of this developed after the 1979 revolution, Iranian students at all levels of education were already very present in Western universities in the 1970s.[4]

Applying the grammar

In Figure 7, both the top and bottom arrows are now out of the italics that signify blocks because my discovery of the cosmopolitan and

---

4 See *Encyclopaedia Iranica* entry vii, https://www.iranicaonline.org/articles/diaspora#pt8.

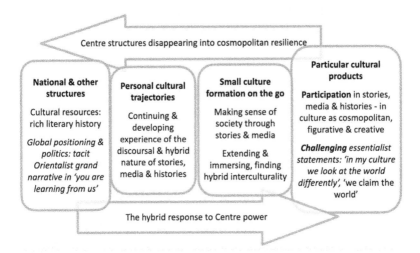

Figure 7 Grammar of culture (stories and media).

hybrid nature of stories and histories in Iran did indeed dissolve the power of Centre structures. The true nature of culture as figurative, flowing, and creative succeeded in pulling away from the divisive 'us'- 'them' Orientalist imagination.

The statement about culture not in italics (bottom right) relates to the Iranian appropriation of world stories and histories, 'claiming the world', that shakes the normal essentialism of difference. From my perspective, all of this appreciation of a deeper, hybrid cosmopolitan meaning (centre right) is enabled by my cultural resources of similar stories and histories (left centre) and a development that continued into the future (centre left). This was also a major shaking of the Orientalist grand narrative that brought me up to believe that it was only Westerners who had the right to travel.

The Orientalist grand narrative does however not completely go away (bottom left) because there is still the sustained sense that all of the cosmopolitanism observed in the other domains could have been learned from the West, which in turn feeds the essentialist statements about culture still in italics (bottom right).

7 Combatting the emergence of native-speakerism

In this final chapter, I will show how the context of working at the British Council as an English teacher provided a particular further contextualisation for my sense-making about living in Iran. There was some sort of disjunct between my own experience of how learning Farsi interfaced with hybrid social realities and what I was beginning to imagine about my students learning English from the perspective of a developing native-speakerism within my professional domain. As I write now, it becomes clear that this native-speakerism is in fact an ideological projection of the Orientalist grand narrative.

Linguaculture

In Chapter 4, I observed that learning the language, while an absolute necessity, came second to and followed instrumentally from learning how to travel by taxi. In Chapter 6, I observed that access to Iranian stories and histories was as much through stories and histories in English as through Farsi. While language had to be acquired for everyday communication, including watching television and reading street signs and advertisements, where a shared semiotics came into use, much of my daily communication was with friends, colleagues, and students in English, but with Iranian cultural reference and demeanour.

Speaking English with an Iranian 'demeanour', and indeed Farsi with an English demeanour can best be explained through Risager's concept of linguaculture. Referring to herself as a Dane, says that 'people carry their Danish language resources with them into new cultural contexts and perhaps put them to use in new ways under new circumstances', and that this is evident when they speak different languages (2020: 115). She is therefore able to say, 'I tend to build on my Danish linguaculture, when I speak English, French or German' (p. 121). This helps to explain how my Englishness was therefore

DOI: 10.4324/9781003039174-7

carried into Farsi as a mechanism for being myself in a culturally new environment, while Farsiness was also carried back into the English I used with those who spoke it. This means that even if I was not able to use my English, its linguaculture would have been present in my greater use of Farsi in the process of me being myself in a genuine and hybrid relationship with the Iranian people that I encountered.

A particular example is how my experience of Arabic script in Farsi also enhanced my conceptualisation of script in English. This thought was introduced to me by my informant, Irene, who was learning Japanese. She told me that experiencing Japanese characters made her see and experience Italian in different ways. Whether or not I was using it with other Iranian people, my English would never be the same again. This is the recollection of a process of awareness over time and into the present:

> Although I never became remotely fluent in reading or writing, I became acutely aware of the physical appearance of the script as it was represented in signs and fragments of handwriting that I saw around me. I noted, for example, how the ends of lines and their relationship with margins were managed in handwriting with extended letters and sub-script and margin notes. The particular fluidity of the script allowed for words to be pulled, curved and threaded to literally create tapestries and weaves. At a time before social media, when handwriting on paper was seen everywhere.
>
> This was much more than like seeing images of fragments of Leonardo Da Vinci's script almost drawn alongside his technical illustrations, or the latter seeming to have been written like his script - or perhaps even seeing one's own handwriting in the mirror.

This seeing of form and metastructure over content, which then informed my understanding of the more familiar, was similar to that experienced in watching theatre, soap opera, and satirical comedy as described in Chapter 6.

As a novice language teacher at that time, I was not so influenced by the growth of the association between a so-called communicative revolution and an essentialist view that learning a language meant learning its culture as though the two mapped precisely onto each other. My learning of Farsi was not therefore hindered by any barriers in this respect. Though there were some Orientalist aspects. The highly behaviourist form of English teaching that I was practising at the time, did help me to understand the nature of learning language behaviour as small culture formation on the go. One might refer to this as small *language* formation on the go. The implication here was that the language followed instrumentally from learning small cultural practices through direct observation. However, these were not so much particular bounded practices, but a continuation of behavioural processes. Therefore, I was not simply learning the language repertoire as it was limited within the boundaries of, for example, the taxis and the edges of the pavements where they stopped for passengers. It was a broader repertoire I was beginning to acquire informed by the stories, media and histories that I was making sense of elsewhere. This also confirmed the hybridity of language in the same way as the hybridity of all the relationships I was forming (Holliday 2021b; Mahboob 2015; Rajagopalan 2012; Saraceni 2015; Schneider 2016).

Pre-native-speakerism

Nevertheless, within the context of my sense of professionalism as a teacher at the British Council, this hybrid and open notion of language was tempted back to essentialist, Centre structures. As I was not aware of the Orientalist grand narrative at this time, I was also hardly aware of the significance of the changing fault lines of my profession that I was witnessing. I am referring to this moment as pre-native-speakerist because, although it was after the what Phillipson (1992) has described as the birth of the idealisation of the so-labelled 'native speaker' English teacher as a saleable commodity of postcolonial dominance across the world, it did not really arrive at the British Council teaching centre in Tehran until just after I arrived.

The seeds of native-speakerism were nevertheless there, very much embodied in my presence. I was not aware of this at the time, not knowing about the full force of native-speakerism that was to come in parallel development to my own career, which I since wrote about in some detail (Holliday 2005). Looking back now, and informed by the realisations about the conflict between a brought Orientalist grand narrative and found hybrid modernity that I have developed in writing this book, I see this conflict being acted out in my beginning teaching of English.

I was employed as a part-time teacher. I had a postgraduate certificate in education for teaching history and English as a first language, had taught these subjects at a secondary school in London for a year and had taught English as a foreign language in private language schools over two summers. There is no doubt that my ease of employment in Iran was because I was labelled as a 'native speaker'.

There were also backpackers and spouses whose only 'qualification' was this native-speakerist label; and it was my determination not to be associated with them that drew me to a professional identity what was already framing students 'from other cultures' according to the native-speakerist notion that they needed to be taught how to learn. I can now see the connection between this false narrative about a culturally deficient 'non-native speaker' Other and the Orientalist grand narrative-inspired West as steward discourse (Holliday 2019: 128–129; Holliday & Amadasi 2020: 17–20) in which 'we' in West need to 'help' the world to think and learn. Hence this reconstructed account in my 2005 book:

> In the middle of one of my lessons, an Iranian man who must have been in his 40s or 50s stood up at the back of the classroom, apologised for interrupting in this way and asked me if I could explain the grammar underlying the language structure I was asking him to repeat. I put him down rather abruptly by saying that in 'these classes' he did not need to think about grammar and that to do so would get in the way of his learning. I thought the request was unscientific and unnecessary, and showed the lack of understanding of 'how to learn' that I expected from Iranian students. More than this, but connected, I though his whole manner was ridiculous because he translated directly from a Farsi expression of politeness and had not even realised that this was inappropriate in English.
>
> (Holliday 2005: 56)

This abrupt putting down of a man much older than myself because he was not confirming to the methodology for learning that only I, the professional teacher, could impart was in stark contrast to a very different I was seeing around me but perhaps not seeing the importance of.

Iranian teachers and the ownership of English

In my first year, my memory is that the majority of the teachers at the British Council were Iranian, including the senior teacher who first observed and assessed my teaching. In sharp contrast to my assumption about the students in my lesson above, this account assumes a far more inclusive approach:

> Pirooz was a senior Iranian teacher who had a particularly creative and energetic view about how English should be taught and

learnt. He was often heard to say that students needed to be more confident about taking ownership of the language. He said that competence in the language gave the licence to invent new expressions that might never have been heard before - that whatever a competent user of English said or wrote was correct. He was part of a group of experienced Iranian teachers who were my first professional role models and reference group.

I do not wish to use this recollection to get into a discussion about the nature of language learning or use, which is beyond the scope of this book. The significance I wish to draw from this here is that the first person I heard speak about the hybridity of English was not a so-labelled 'native speaker'. In 1973, Pirooz was saying something that I did not personally hear again for another 40 years until Rajagopalan's statement that people should be labelled 'native speakers' of whatever language they use, but that this 'stretching' of the use of the label reveals is 'uselessness and utter dispensability' other than sustaining the 'myth' of 'an openly racist ideology' (2012: 210).

While I was learning from these Iranian teachers about the hybrid mobility of English, I was also experiencing, again without appreciating the importance, the hybrid criticality of my students.

Iranian students and hybrid criticality

The following reconstructed autoethnographic account is based on an assignment which one of my students at the British Council wrote about me.[1] It presents a very different picture of my students to the one I challenged because of his question about grammar above.

Parvaneh was left with feelings of ambivalence by her teacher's behaviour and choices. While she felt that he was a good person and had got used to his mode of teaching, there were some things that she wasn't sure about. This is what led her to write about him in her assignment.

She was a student of engineering in her second year at university and was already pretty sure of getting a place at a university

---

1 I still have the assignment, which is 14 pages long, written in the winter of 1974, but which I cannot cite from directly because of the impossibility of getting permission so many years after the event. The re-constructed ethnographic account also incorporates some material pieced together from my knowledge of students like the writer of the assignment.

in the United States for her masters degree. She nevertheless went to the British Council rather than the Iran-America Society because she wanted a broad cultural experience that would expand her horizons. Her English was already good. She'd re-read in English translation some of the Russian and French classics that she loved in Farsi translation. She found the 'humanities' atmosphere at the British Council a different sort of challenge to the rigours of her engineering course. She liked the discussions in the British Council classes, the extensive library of novels and drama, and sitting in the beautiful garden having coffee and cake with other students from different backgrounds and sometimes her teachers.

This particular teacher was though strangely aloof outside class. While generally his classes were stimulating and she enjoyed them tremendously, some of the stories he brought for them to discuss were a bit lacking in intellectual content. He also sometimes seemed to be strangely misunderstanding of who his students were, which was strange to her considering that his wife was Iranian. At the same time, it was the mysteries of her teachers that she also enjoyed.

There was however one incident that really got to her. For some reason he decided to have a class debate about the proposition that Iranian women were only interested in getting married. The choice of topic immediately caused a bit of a stir in the class. It was certainly a topic that was in the air; but more as a common prejudice than a truth. Some of the students felt a bit insulted that the topic somehow implied that it was a prejudice to do with being Iranian.

When the debate took place, Parvaneh volunteered to speak against the motion. She intended to say that she thought it was a prejudice about women across the world, and wanted to cite a novel she'd been reading. But then, the worst of all things happened. She couldn't say a word. She attributed this to the pressures on women expressing their voices on certain topics in Iranian society, which she found depressing. She didn't though want her foreign teacher to get the wrong impression about this.

She did though take the opportunity to write about this experience of ambivalence about her teacher and what happened in the debate in an assignment that they were set over the Christmas break. She was cautious to ask her teacher if this was appropriate. She interpreted *his* apparent ambivalence as permission. Despite her embarrassment at feeling silenced in the debate, she took the courage to write about it in detail along with her ambivalence about him.

As with a number of accounts in this book, this one can be read in different ways. The Orientalist perspective would see it simply as evidence of oppression of individualism and move on. It might be argued that Parvaneh herself supports this view when she refers to the pressures of Iranian society.

The other reading is that Parvaneh is in common with women *even* in the West who feel intimidated by male voices in classrooms, meetings and other scenarios. This reading is supported by her clear hybrid modernity, none of which is surprising once the Orientalist grand narrative is put aside. Being well-read resonates with Russian novels in Simin's book case in Chapter 6 and her personal choice to study at the British Council because of its environment, and her criticality regarding the way in which she is being taught, within the perspective of already going to the United States, make her no different from students everywhere who are worldly and discerning. (Being an engineering student is significant because I remember very well having learned the common prejudice among Western professionals that Iranian engineering was just about theory, with no practical application.) Within this interpretation, Parvaneh associating her silence with Iranian society does not mean that Iranian society is special in this respect – i.e. not that this is an exclusive feature of collectivist 'Iranian culture'.

When I try to work out why I, as the teacher, decided to have a debate on 'Iranian women only want marriage', I think that I probably thought it to be a topical subject that would encourage discussion for the purpose of practising the language. This may seem innocent – as what all English teachers do to enable practice of the language. However, now, just as I am convinced that Parvaneh's feeling unable to speak was *not* an exclusive feature of 'Iranian culture', I can see that my choice of the topic was very likely to do with a false, Orientalist, imagination that 'they' needed something controversial to 'get them to talk and express critical opinions' – as if they would not know how to talk and critique without my Western teacherly intervention.

My attention is drawn to the easy-to-miss ideological framing of the classroom debate by Lowe's (2020: 122) observation that the requirements for classroom discussion in a Japanese university English course represented 'a native-speakerist discourse about the perceived deficiencies of students' is 'that the students needed to be trained in how to communicate – not just in English, but in general'. While Lowe observed that the students were already perfectly capable of discussing in both English and Japanese and did not need the teaching that the course required, he noted a teacher saying that 'the biggest issue in the course was "to get them [students] to have ideas in the first place"' (his insertion).

I simply did not appreciate that my students' hybrid criticality, even in silence, was probably way ahead of mine. Parvaneh's assignment, in its acute observation and reflective searching for meaning, also written excellently in English, is clear evidence that she was in no way bound by an imagined collectivist culture in which individualist ideas and critical opinion are hard to find.

Normal preoccupation and classroom presence

What Parvaneh teaches me is that the contradictions in her assignment are not about large, civilisational culture differences but about the small differences, preoccupations, and uncertainties that surround all of us all the time. They are the everyday material of small culture formation on the go; and we need to see them as small.

One such small culture 'on the go' explanation can be applied to me not saying hello to students outside class in Parvaneh's assignment:

> Me not saying hello outside class was part of my natural reserve; but also brought along by a piece of advice from my friend Mahnaz before going to the British Council for the first time – that Iranians expected teachers to be very formal and to never smile or be too friendly in the class if I want to maintain respect. I felt this went too much against my experience of teaching so far and so did not take too much notice. However, I mixed this up with my sense of professionalism – with my determination not to be associated with people who were employed as teachers because they were so-labelled 'native speakers'. I wanted to be recognised as a trained professional; and therefore didn't say hello outside the class.
>
> Then I read in Parvaneh's assignment the place where she says that her mother told her that she should be like 'English girls', very polite, not laughing too much, wearing long skirts below the knee and 'frugal in time and money'. She then said that she didn't necessarily agree with her mother, but that it was an image to be considered. I, though, read this to mean that I was somehow expected to be reserved.

These references to reserve are on the one hand examples of essentialist blocks because they fit well-known stereotypes. However, there are other realities in the account that do not fit the stereotype. There is ambivalence in Parvaneh's assignment which implies that students certainly did not want me to be reserved and 'frugally' formal. It needs to be remembered that Mahnaz, Parvaneh, her mother, and I, are just individual people with opinions. These opinions are indeed splintered down from the Orientalist grand narrative that separates the constructed 'simple honesty' of the Protestant European from the 'extravagance' of the imagined East; but Parvaneh's hybrid criticality shows that they can be more than this.

My reading of critical ambivalence in Parvaneh's assignment continues in its reference to the physicality of my presence in the classroom:

> At the beginning of the assignment was a drawing of me writing on the blackboard in the square room. The room is furnished with brown wooden chairs with wooden study arms. They are quite substantial and heavy. Completely in defiance of Mahnaz's advice, Parvaneh describes how I sit on the back of the chair with my feet on the seat and swing a little. She describes how another student stops her from sitting on a chair because I've had my feet on it and the seat is dusty.

There is some resonance here with Mahnaz's comment in Chapter 5 that Iranians often watch out for each other in public places. There is also a particular attention to cleanliness that I also feel I have begun to acquire because of my time in Iran. What Parvaneh chooses to notice indeed might be different to what Mahnaz notices the British people in the car choose to notice in Chapter 5. There are indeed cultural flows here that make a difference, but not that lock us in large cultural blocks of division.

The ambivalence continues in my memory of how I wanted to present myself and was received in people's homes:

> When I went to people's homes to give private lessons, to supplement my part-time employment at the British Council in the first year, I was always purposefully late because I assumed that they would respect me more for this. However, when I got there they often rejected my intention to teach structured 'lessons' with and said they just wanted to practise conversation.

I do not recall any response from the students about my time keeping. It certainly seemed wise always to go to their homes, rather than for them to come to mine, so that I could be more in control of the beginning and finishing of the lesson. My far longer professional experience after this time can certainly attest to the diversity of time-keeping practices regardless of which part of the world people came from.

What was, however, very evident, in almost every case, was my miscalculation regarding what the students wanted me to do during 'the lesson' – which was *not* to go through a structured textbook. They did not need me to show them 'how to learn'. If I had this time again, I would, very professionally, guide the 'conversation' they wanted to 'build on the heuristics' they brought with them, as so well described years later by Kumaravadivelu (1993), in the hybrid modernity I increasingly found amongst them.

The following case of a virtuoso musician may seem an extreme example. However, in so many ways, while I might have been helping them with English, all my private students were introducing me not just to Iran but to the wider world of which Iranian people claimed ownership:

> One of my students was a nationally famous and iconic composer and violinist. He was the uncle of Simin's friend. He was a larger-than-life person; and there was no way that I could in any way impose my professionalism upon him. So I let him set the agenda. He basically wanted someone to speak English with and to be corrected when he made mistakes. Most important for me was the personal introduction I got to the Iranian classical music world. He gave me three audio cassette recordings of him playing, sometimes accompanying iconic women singers, one of whom was his 'wife before'. He made me feel that I was becoming part of the cultural life of the country.

'Cultural life' is another phrase that helps re-capture the figurative aspect of culture that crosses boundaries and helped me connect with the developing interest in European classical music that I brought with me. My student's music was also 'classical' and helped me gain a deeper understanding of what this meant – a wider and more critical perspective on the meaning of 'classical'.

Lingering pre-native-speakerism regarding 'correct' language use

This iconic composer's use of 'wife before' connects with another example of ambivalence between my projected professionalism and the hybridity I was surrounded by. The phrase is an example of uses of English which I always felt I needed to correct because they did not conform to my concept of so-labelled 'native speaker' language. One such item of phraseology which I initially felt attacked my sense of personal identity was how I was addressed. However, there was also some movement here, which resonates with my learning about the deeper recognition of personal space in Chapter 3:

> I felt initially quite annoyed that even my close friends referred to me as 'Mr Adrian'. However, I got used in Farsi to always placing some sort of title or honorific, like 'dear', in front of people's names when I spoke to them. I always used this with close friends, even when speaking in front of others. Although I did not use these phrases outside Farsi, knowledge of them somehow made me more aware of everyone's personal status and when and how this needed to be acknowledged.[2]

It is only in recent years that this understating of the use of honorifics in Farsi and some other languages has led me to change my position regarding honorifics used by students who come to Britain from other places to study. There was a time when I would 'correct' them for addressing me as 'Professor Holliday' or 'Professor Adrian' instead of the British academic norm of 'Adrian'. I misunderstood this as a mistake with regard to formality and informality rather than alternative ways of expressing appreciation of self. I now feel the need to recognise boundary-dissolving hybridity in this respect. This also relates to the speaking about other things before getting down to business that I also found initially so annoying in Chapter 3. I now also feel the need to make some sort of personal contact at the beginning of a work conversation. While this may not be the perceived norm in many workplaces in the so-labelled West, it is often appreciated as long as the timing is right. Also, it is always good to disturb the norm.

Images of hybrid modernity and English

The full significance of what Parvaneh wrote in her assignment, above, did not occur to me until I began to write this autoethnography; and

---

2 Adapted from the 'John abroad, politeness and space' reconstructed ethnographic account which is based on my experience in Iran (Holliday 2019: 166–167) where there is further discussion.

I make sense of it further in juxtaposition with my observation of what was on the bookshelf in Simin's home in Chapter 6. The third space that these observations take me into makes me also think again about the English language textbook, *Present day English for foreign students* (Candlin 1968), that I also saw on Simin's bookshelf. In my beginning persona as an English teacher, I may have judged it on what was becoming considered a dated use of content that was too bland to motivate learning. Each unit exemplifies new language through descriptions of British life, each with a single monochrome drawing, a conversation, and language exercises.

This was quite different to what was regarded as the more 'communicative' textbook that was introduced a few years after I arrived – *Strategies* (Abbs & Freebairn 1975). This new type of book's dense collage of authentic-looking textual material such as letters, newspaper articles, reports, and shopping lists, with multiple fonts and graphics, is designed for 'role-playing, improvisation, simulation, and co-operative problem-solving or task-based work' (Howatt & Smith 2014: 90). While some work hard to promote gender and ethnic equality (Rixon & Smith 2012: 390, referring to Abbs & Freebairn), such books have been much critiqued for their seductively hard sell of particular branded images of the Western cultural Self (Gray 2010; Kullman 2013). It is also no coincidence that *Strategies* arrived in the British Council at the same time as the so-labelled 'native speaker' senior teachers mentioned earlier. The hard sell of so-labelled 'native speaker' English in 'communicative' classroom activities came powerfully with Orientalist cultural implications of 'learning' individualist thought processes. Hence Gray's (2010: 729) reference to 'the British Council's 2003 recruitment campaign – "Teach English and Individualism"'.

I mention this to help make sense of Parvaneh and Simin as students of English who had no need of all of this. Another clue is Canagarajah's (1999: 90) well-cited report of how Sri Lankan school children resist the imperialist influence of their American textbook by privately writing into it their own cultural stories. Similarly, in Gong and Holliday (2013: 47–48), Chinese school children in rural areas resist the false belief that 'critical choice' is only present in 'Western culture' practices of ordering pizza in fast-food restaurants and planning holidays abroad of which they had no experience. They were already capable of making critical choices in such daily activities as picking vegetables and cooking for themselves while their parents were working away from home. In the same world-claiming mode as observed in events in this book, they ask for a different textbook content that would enable them to engage with bigger world issues such as 'love, politics, and life skills'.

I was able to talk to Simin about this at the time of writing this book:

> Simin told me that she thought that *Present day English* was so interesting – the characters, how they went about their lives, and the events and the places that they went to. She felt that it connected to her life at the time that she was using it in high school, before she travelled to Britain. She said that she wasn't one of the rich girls in her school who had already been to Europe or the United States, but that she felt that this didn't prevent her from having a critical viewpoint about what she saw in the book. She didn't find anything shocking or particularly alien about the places or the characters depicted there.

When I look at the content of the textbook, I can see why she would not find 'shocking' or 'alien' content. While it is set in British settings, most of them are things that also go on in Iranian urban life, for example 'wallpaper and paint', 'a visit to a factory', 'an evening at the cinema' and 'a family birthday' (Candlin 1968: 9, 60, 106, 134), but with different cultural flavour – sometimes different looking streets, buildings, uniforms, names and so on. It is the same sort of resonance that Doshi, cited in Chapter 6, sees between Indian and Welsh family gatherings. It is like what I have worked out in this book. If I had not heard the Orientalist rumours that Iranian 'culture' 'has' widely different, 'collectivist' values to my 'individualist' ones, I would not have noticed them as such.

There was also another dimension to Simin's understanding:

> I asked Simin what it was that helped her to connect with places that she'd never been to, especially given that there was no internet or social media at that time to bring her instant images. In answer, she didn't refer to the sub-titled Hollywood movies or American television that she'd seen. Instead she replied that she'd read Dostoyevsky.

The grammar applied

Thinking about how to populate the grammar of culture in Figure 8 in response to the events in this chapter leads me to find more connections that I had not previously thought of.

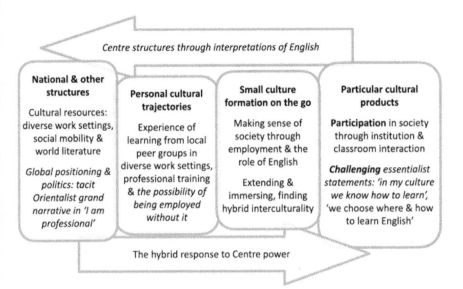

Figure 8 Grammar of culture (language, concepts, and classrooms).

The block is back in the top arrow when compared with the experience in Chapter 6, meaning that this has something to do with the institutional context, the classroom, and the centrality of English within it, which is the focus of small culture formation on the go (right middle of the figure). The blocking elements that contribute are in italics in the essentialist statements about culture that 'we know how to learn' (bottom right). This is my initial retort to the student who I challenged for asking about grammar and also behind my preference for how I should teach private students. It is also splintered from the Orientalist grand narrative which claims monopoly of this professionalism (bottom left). There is also the irony in my asserting my professionalism because of the possibility that I am employed simply because I am labelled a 'native speaker' (both left middle).

The hybrid opposition to these essentialist blocks (bottom arrow) is nevertheless powerful in its success in pushing me on to a broader understanding throughout the chapter. There is a competing thread in the statements about culture, 'we choose' (bottom right). I also here recall, as a result of reflecting on the grammar, in the moment of reverie that it invites, my experience of other work settings that have appeared initially very foreign (centre right). Being able to treat the Iranian teachers as my reference group resonates with fellow hospital porters and shop assistants when I worked in a hospital and a department store while being a university student. In many ways they were as different to me, through class and upbringing, as were the Iranian teachers. This possibility of diversity of work was also generally a resource that I brought with me (right top).

The other cultural resource which provided a major route to my eventually seeing the hybrid modernity of the people around me was the Russian novels that I recalled from Simin's bookshelf in Chapter 6, which opened my eyes to the ambivalent criticality that Parvaneh brought to me in her assignment and enabled a re-reading of the English language textbook also on Simin's bookshelf.

8 Finding hybrid integration

At the end of a book that recalls staying in Iran for six years, the question that will emerge in at least some readers' minds will be that of integration. What I believe I have implicitly argued against is the idea of embracing the practices and values of what might be termed a 'host culture', where the eventual aim might be some sort of assimilation.[1]

Critiquing assimilation

A parody of this essentialist ideal is in the *Star trek* science fiction television series where the alien Borg assimilates humans by incorporating them into a central artificial intelligence and deleting their 'humanity'. Fraser's (2008) newspaper article refers to this. He cites an extract from a then-recent British government statement that minority ethnic groups need to integrate more:

> For too long, too many people in this country have been living parallel lives, refusing to integrate and failing to embrace the shared values that make Britain great.

His critique follows:

> [This] approach reminds me of one of the great *Star trek* villains: 'We are the Borg. Lower your shields and surrender your ships. We will add your biological and technological distinctiveness to our own. Your culture will adapt to service us. Resistance is futile.' The Borg have a hive mind, scouring the galaxy for people

1 There is a discussion of the issues with integration in Holliday and Amadasi (2020: 31–34) and Kumaravadivelu (2007: 5).

DOI: 10.4324/9781003039174-8

who think and live differently in order to subsume them into their own way of being.

While there is a sense here that the Borg might be enriched by incorporating diverse others, their victims suffer the 'loss' of their own 'cultures' because, being also bounded and essentialist, they cannot exist as parts of someone else's. This view is expressed by Mina in Chapter 5 feeling that 'her culture' has no place in Western streets.

One might suggest that Fraser's article is only to do with migrant groups and ethnic minorities rather than with people like me travelling to Iran to work as an 'expatriate' – i.e. living temporarily in another country because their job or leisure pursuits take them there – perhaps associated with 'white privilege and the persistence of colonial power' (Kunz 2019). However, unlike the British Council teachers who were employed from London. On the basis that we believed I would have better career opportunities there, I was an economic migrant.

The example of me in Iran is however just one instance in a huge diversity of why and how different types of people live in countries other than where they or their recent generations were born. So-labelled international students are also living abroad for short periods of time to carry out particular activities. If we put aside the Orientalist grand narrative, studying in a Western university does *not* require learning what has falsely been presumed to be an alien mode of individualist-independent thinking. If we put aside the native-speakerism that follows the Orientalist grand narrative, as I have tried to do in Chapter 7, neither does learning the language require this imagined cultural shift. This then removes the need for much of the anxiety about how and when they 'mix' with 'domestic' students, as expressed nicely by Osmond and Roed (2009).

A more open engagement

Some sort of integration is however a good thing if it can be instead defined as an open set of different types of engagement from taking an interest in one's surroundings and the people there and their practices and values to different types of active engagement. I do feel that it is good if my students from other countries get involved in whatever aspects of British life they feel attracted to, simply for the purpose of taking the opportunity to find the threads that I have demonstrated in this book that connect aspects of social life in multiple scenarios. This does not however mean that they need to be 'taught', on the basis of where they come from, any more than British students, about how to engage. Perhaps all students might need it to be drawn to their attention that direct observation of life around them has relevance to whatever they are studying (Holliday 2021a).

This diversity of engagement is very evident in Sadoudi's (forthcoming) study of Algerian students 'travelling to the West'. Despite polarised views derived from an idealised grand narrative of the West they had been brought up with, there was evidence that they:

> succeeded in finding their own creative ways of overcoming those challenges and being themselves without trying to integrate or assimilate. This is because, as the data showed, home is not a country; it does not have borders. Home is not a place, but rather a feeling. Participants' accounts appear to indicate that they felt home even in places where they have never been before without having to assimilate. ... Each of them had a different lifestyle, different hobbies and friendship patterns, and gave the impression of blending into the society's fabric regardless of their provenance. I believe that the ability of feeling home and being able to find oneself even in unfamiliar terrains represent what being intercultural really is.

Her reference to finding oneself even in unfamiliar terrains also resonates back to my definition of the intercultural in Chapter 1 with regard to how we are made to position and reposition ourselves, and in different ways at different times depending on multiple circumstances. In her thesis, Sadoudi very skilfully shows us the details of the diversity of circumstances that govern the particularities of how and why each of the students engages. Her redefining the meaning of 'home' to meet this openness also resonates with my definition of culture as figurative.

This finding ways of being one's self is a theme of Chapters 4 and 5, where I realise that any form of imitation of imagined Iranian practices and values would be highly inappropriate and not be taken seriously within the discovered cosmopolitan diversity of Iranian society. This sense of authentic Self is also searched for in Parvaneh's critical essay about me as a teacher in Chapter 7. This is also at the core of the notion of 'hybrid integration' defined by Baraldi (2019) as being able to 'exercise agency in constructing their identities and changing their social contexts' and 'negotiation' of 'hybrid identities'.

The possibility of hybrid integration has enabled an opening up in the understanding of children with migration backgrounds in European education settings.[2] It resonates strongly with the discussion in this book because finding it requires the same struggle against prevailing large-culture blocks about the fixity of childhood (Baraldi & Iervese 2017: 403). Project facilitators therefore had to apply creative workshop methods to allow the children's personal narratives to become visible (p. 404) which I put under the heading of deCentred third-space methodology.

This hard work in looking differently at things enables an interculturality which is a boundary-dissolving finding of Self in Other and Other in Self. This, by its nature, however, needs to be a deep, complex, difficult and often even political experience (Dervin 2016). Unseating large-culture blocks is indeed political because it moves against the Centre orientation of the internationally constructed order. It is by no means looking from one large culture to be tolerant of another large culture, where tolerance implies putting up with something which is essentially different to us and will eventually lead to prejudice. In this sense, my discussion about being in Iran in this book, while purposely looking at the fluidity and hybridity of small intercultural things on the go, even though in a pre-revolutionary and therefore very different order to the present, is also a political statement because it allows for the everyday voices of ordinary people to run beyond how they are ideologically framed by nation-state governments. This sentiment is expressed by Bayat (1997: xi–xii) in his rationale for writing about the 'street politics' of 'ordinary' Iranian people as contrast to the grand narrative media images of 'fanaticism' related to the 1979 Iranian revolution.

The implication of choice among the students in Sadoudi's thesis, above, and how far they manage to resist false grand narratives about the West, is at the core of the transience of small culture formation on the go which and can lead to legitimate decisions not to participate. That this does not however endorse a free-for-all is evident in the definite exception I took in Chapter 5 to the two American soldiers in the taxi seemingly completely disregarding their surroundings except to criticise. I also observed the hugely patronising and negative effect of between-the-lines essentialist, Orientalist, Western judgement. Such negativity encourages the large-culture blocks that would have prevented my appreciating that Iranian people do *not* deny personal

2 This is the basis of the Horizon 2020 CHILD-UP project – 'Children Hybrid Integration: Learning Dialogue as a way of Upgrading policies of Participation' – http://www.child-up.eu.

space in Chapter 3 and do *not* need special classroom strategies to be 'made to' speak and think critically in Chapter 7. Integration is therefore *not* about learning practices and values that are rumoured by large-culture grand narratives. It is instead the result of researching, looking around with deCentred, third-space interrogation for both Other and Self.

Opening unexpected hybridities

Whether or not we are completely successful in the third-space struggle to put aside false large-culture grand narratives, a deCentred understanding of the intercultural undoubtedly begins to emerge. Just as a result of writing this book I have begun to see what I had not seen before – to become even more appreciative of perhaps unnoticed corners of intercultural experience.

It would however be a great mistake, in pushing aside the large-culture trope and the grand narratives that promote it, if cultural difference and diversity were also pushed aside. There is something very particularly Iranian about the people I encounter, but it is not an Iranianness that can be packaged into a large-culture description. Each Iranian, each British person, is also completely different to every other Iranian and British person. This is the basis of hybridity – that, in the many things we are, we also do have complex national identities.

What I hope that I have been able to open up in the book is creative diversity beyond large-culture fixity. I make passing reference in Chapter 1 to the impossible-to-understand third script of Persian mystic, Shams-e Tabrizi. The conundrum of how we can all be different in very different ways and also the same without defining boundaries between us remains. The major principle must be that we really *must stop* trying to explain and judge people based on *a priori* large-culture grand narratives (whether people are Western, Eastern, British, Chinese or Italian) in the same way as we are learning not to judge or explain on the basis of gender or the imagined category of race.

It is following the inspiration of Simin and Parvaneh reading Russian novels that I recall again reading Homer's *Iliad* perhaps at the age of 18, while sitting above Tarn Hows in the Lake District in the North of England where I was brought up. The location gives special meaning to the imagination that my ancestors were the ancient Greeks, as discussed in Chapter 2. But this does not mean that I should allow this connection to drive me to Orientalism. It should remain where it belongs—a figurative, creative, flowing cultural reference that enables me to be part of the world. The removal of an Orientalist myth that 'they' are 'all the same' in their traditions and 'we' are 'individuals' in ours should enable all of us to understand the idiosyncratic individuality of everyone.

Bibliography

Abbs, B., & Freebairn, I. (1975). *The strategies series.* Longman.

Adams, D. (1979). *The hitchiker's guide to the galaxy.* Pan Books.

Agar, M. (1990). Text and fieldwork: 'Exploring the excluded middle'. *Journal of Contemporary Ethnography, 19*(1), 73–88.

Amadasi, S. (2010). *La doppia presenza. Pratiche transnazionali tra Senegal e Italia* (PhD thesis). Università di Modena e Reggio Emilia.

Amadasi, S. (2020). "He was as if on the moon". The relevance of narratives told by teachers in the understanding of transnational experiences lived by children. *Italian Journal of Sociology of Education, 12*(1), 226–248.

Amadasi, S., & Holliday, A. R. (2017). Block and thread intercultural narratives and positioning: conversations with newly arrived postgraduate students. *Language & Intercultural Communication, 17*(3), 254–269.

Anderson, B. (2006a). *Imagined communities* (2nd ed.). Verso.

Anderson, L. (2006b). Analytic autoethnography. *Journal of Contemporary Ethnography, 35*(4), 373–395.

Andrić, I. (1995). *Bridge over the Drina* (L. F. Edwards, Trans.). Harvill Press.

Antonsich, M., Cantle, T., Modood, T., & Iacovino, R. (2016). Interculturalism versus multiculturalism – The Cantle-Modood debate. *Ethnicities, 16*(3), 470–493.

Atkinson, P. (2006). Rescuing autoethnography. *Journal of Contemporary Ethnography, 35*(4), 400–404.

Badwan, K. (2021). *Language in a globalised world: social justice perspectives on mobility and contact.* Palgrave Macmillan.

Badwan, K., & Hall, E. (2020). Walking along in sticky places: post-humanist and affective insights from a reflective account of two young women in Manchester, UK. *Language & Intercultural Communication, 20*(3), 225–239.

Baraldi, C. (2019). *The child-centred approach of CHILD-UP project.* Paper presented at the Migrant Children and Communities in a Transforming Europe: Migrant Children'S Integration and Education in Europe, Barcelona.

Baraldi, C., & Iervese, V. (2017). Narratives of memories and dialogue in multicultural classrooms: analysis of workshops based on the use of photography. *Narrative Inquiry, 27*(2), 398–417.

Barnes, J. M. (2014). Interdisciplinary, praxis-focused auto-ethnography: using autobiography and the values discussion to build capacity in teachers. *Advances in Social Sciences Research Journal*, 1(5), 160–182.

Baumann, G. (1996). *Contesting culture*. Cambridge University Press.

Bayat, A. (1997). *Street politics: poor people's movements in Iran*. Columbia University Press.

Bayat, A. (2008). Everyday cosmopolitanism. *ISIM Review*, 22(1), 5–5.

Beck, U., & Sznaider, N. (2006). Unpacking cosmopolitanism for the social sciences: a research agenda. *British Journal of Sociology*, 57(1), 1–23.

Berger, P., & Luckmann, T. (1966/1979). *The social construction of reality*. Penguin.

Bhabha, H. K. (1992). The world and the home. *Social Text*, 31(32), 141–153.

Bhabha, H. K. (1994). *The location of culture*. Routledge.

Blackman, S. J., & Kempson, M. (2017). Introduction. In S. J. Blackman & M. Kempson (Eds.), *The subcultural imagination: theory, research and reflexivity in contemporary youth cultures*. Routledge.

Bolten, J. (2014). The dune model – or: how to describe cultures. *AFS Intercultural Link*, 5(2), 4–6.

Borger, J. (2020). British spy's account sheds light on role in 1953 Iranian coup. *The Guardian*. Retrieved from https://www.theguardian.com/world/2020/aug/17/british-spys-account-sheds-light-on-role-in-1953-iranian-coup

Borghetti, C. (2016). Intercultural education in practice: two pedagogical experiences with mobile students. *Language and Intercultural Communication*, 16(3), 502–513.

Botting, F. (1995). Culture, subjectivity and the real; or, psychoanalysis reading postmodernity. In B. Adam & S. Allan (Eds.), *Theorising culture: an interdisciplinary critique after postmodernism* (pp. 87–99). UCL Press.

Bragg, M. (2016). *Northern power: speaking from the North*. BBC.

Canagarajah, A. S. (1999). *Resisting linguistic imperialism*. Oxford University Press.

Candlin, E. F. (1968). *Present day English for foreign students*. University of London Press.

Carr, C. E. (2017). *The Spartan boy and the fox: a story*. Quatr.us Study Guides.

Caruana, V. (2014). Re-thinking global citizenship in Higher Education: from cosmopolitanism and international mobility to cosmopolitanisation, resilience and resilient thinking. *Higher Education Quarterly*, 68(1), 85–104.

Caruana, V., & Montgomery, C. (2015). Understanding the transnational higher education landscape: shifting positionality and the complexities of partnership. *Learning & Teaching*, 8(1), 5–29.

Clifford, J., & Marcus, G. E. (Eds.). (1986). *Writing culture: the poetica of politics of ethnography*. University of California Press.

Davies, S. (2011). The Pleasure Seekers by Tishani Doshi: passages from India to Wales. *The Independent*. Retrieved from https://www.independent.co.uk/arts-entertainment/books/reviews/the-pleasure-seekers-by-tishani-doshi-1985571.html

Danius, S., & Jonsson, S. (1993). An interview with Gayatri Chakravorty Spivak. *Boundary*, 20(2), 24–50.

Deardorff, D. K. (2020). *Manual for developing intercultural competencies: story circles*. Routledge.

Delanty, G. (2006). The cosmopolitan imagination: critical cosmopolitanism and social theory. *British Journal of Sociology*, 57(1), 25–47.

Delanty, G. (2012). The idea of critical cosmopolitanism. In G. Delanty (Ed.), *Routledge international handbook of cosmopolitan studies* (pp. 38–46). Routledge.

Delanty, G., Wodak, R., & Jones, P. (Eds.). (2008). *Identity, belonging and migration*. Liverpool University Press.

Denzin, N. K. (1994). The art and politics of interpretation. In N. K. Denzin & Y. S. Lincoln (Eds.), *A handbook of qualitative research* (pp. 500–515). Sage.

Dervin, F. (2011). A plea for change in research on intercultural discourses: A 'liquid' approach to the study of the acculturation of Chinese students. *Journal of Multicultural Discourses*, 6(1), 37–52.

Dervin, F. (2016). *Interculturality in education*. Palgrave Macmillan.

Doshi, T. (2010). *The pleasure seekers* (Kindle ed.). Bloomsbury.

Driscoll, P., & Holliday, A. R. (2019). Cultural threads in three primary schools: Introducing a critical cosmopolitan frame. *AILA Review*, 32, 64–90.

Durkheim, E. (1893/1964). *The division of labour in society* (G. Simpson, Trans.). Free Press.

Ellis, C., Adams, T. E., & Bochner, A. P. (2011). Autoethnography: an overview. *Forum: Qualitative Social Research*, 12(1). https://doi.org/10.17169/fqs-12.1.1589

Emmerich, R. (1996). *Independence day*. Centropolis Entertainment.

Fairclough, N. (1995). *Critical discourse analysis: the critical study of language*. Addison Wesley Longman.

FitzGerald, E. (1906). *The Rubaiyat of Omar Khayyam, version 4*. Roycroft Shop.

Flam, H., & Bauzamy, B. (2008). Symbolic violence. In G. Delanty, R. Wodak, & P. Jones (Eds.), *Identity, belonging and migration* (pp. 221–240). Liverpool University Press.

Fraser, G. (2008). Assimilation threatens the existence of other cultures. *The Guardian*. Retrieved from https://www.theguardian.com/commentisfree/belief/2016/dec/08/assimilation-threatens-the-existence-of-other-cultures

Furnham, A. (2012). Culture shock. *Journal of Psychology and Education*, 7(1), 9–22.

Geertz, C. (1993). *The interpretation of cultures*. Fontana.

Gellner, E. (1964). *Thought and change*. Weidenfeld & Nicolson.

Ghosh, A. (2015). *Flood of fire*. John Murray.

Goffman, E. (1959/1990). *The presentation of self in everyday life*. Penguin Books.

Gong, Y., & Holliday, A. R. (2013). Cultures of change. In K. Hyland & L. Wong (Eds.), *Innovation and change in English language education* (pp. 44–57). Routledge.

Goodson, I. (2006). The rise of the life narrative. *Teacher Education Quarterly*, 33(4), 7–21.

Gray, J. (2010). The branding of English and the culture of the new capitalism: representations of the world of work in English language textbooks. *Applied Linguistics*, 31(5), 714–733.

Grey, Z. (1912). *Purple sage*. Harper & Brothers.

Grimshaw, T. (2007). Problematising the construct of 'the Chinese learner': insights from ethnographic research. *Educational Studies*, 33, 299–311.

Hall, S. (1991). Old and new identities, old and new ethnicities. In A. D. King (Ed.), *Culture, globalisation and the world-system* (pp. 40–68). Palgrave.

Hall, S. (1996). The question of cultural identity. In S. Hall, D. Held, D. Hubert, & K. Thompson (Eds.), *Modernity: an introduction to modern societies* (pp. 595–634). Blackwell.

Hannerz, U. (1991). Scenarios of peripheral cultures. In A. D. King (Ed.), *Culture, globalisation and the world-system* (pp. 107–128). Palgrave.

Hedayat, S. (1937/1958). *The blind owl*. Grove Press.

Herrera, L. (1992). *Scenes of schooling: inside a girls' school in Cairo*. American University of Cairo Press.

Hervik, P. (2013). Racism, neo-racism. In ENAR (Ed.), *Recycling hatred: racism(s) in Europe today: a dialogue between academics, equality experts and civil society activists* (pp. 43–52). The European Network against Racism.

Hofstede, G. (2003). *Culture's consequences: comparing values, behaviours, institutions and organisations across cultures* (2nd ed.). Sage.

Holliday, A. R. (1994). *Appropriate methodology and social context*. Cambridge University Press.

Holliday, A. R. (2005). *The struggle to teach English as an international language*. Oxford University Press.

Holliday, A. R. (2011). *Intercultural communication and ideology*. Sage.

Holliday, A. R. (2012). Interrogating researcher participation in an interview study of intercultural contribution in the workplace. *Qualitative Inquiry*, 18(6), 504–515.

Holliday, A. R. (2016a). Difference and awareness in cultural travel: negotiating blocks and threads. *Language and Intercultural Communication*, 16(3), 318–331.

Holliday, A. R. (2016b). *Doing and writing qualitative research* (3rd ed.). Sage.

Holliday, A. R. (2016c). Revisiting intercultural competence: small culture formation on the go through threads of experience. *International Journal of Bias, Identity & Diversities in Education*, 1(2), 1–13.

Holliday, A. R. (2019). *Understanding intercultural communication: negotiating a grammar of culture* (2nd ed.). Routledge.

Holliday, A. R. (2020). *Blogs 2013–2020: How it is possible to write - Issues with culture*. adrianholliday.com/books.

Holliday, A. R. (2021a). Learning wherever we are about the people in our research. Retrieved from http://adrianholliday.com/learning-wherever-we-are-about-the-people-in-our-research/

Holliday, A. R. (2021b). Linguaculture, cultural travel, native-speakerism and small culture formation on the go: working up from instances. In R. Rubdy & R. Tupas (Eds.), *Bloomsbury world Englishes* (Vol. II, Ideologies, pp. 101–113). Bloomsbury.

Holliday, A. R., & Amadasi, S. (2020). *Making sense of the intercultural: finding deCentred threads.* Routledge.

Holliday, A. R., & MacDonald, M. N. (2020). Researching the intercultural: intersubjectivity and the problem with postpositivism. *Applied Linguistics,* 41(5), 621–639.

Holliday, S. J. (2016d). The legacy of subalternity and Gramsci's national–popular: populist discourse in the case of the Islamic Republic of Iran. *Third World Quarterly,* 37(5), 917–933.

Holman Jones, S. (2005). Autoethnography: making the personal political. In N. K. Denzin & Y. S. Lincoln (Eds.), *Handbook of qualitative research* (3rd ed., pp. 763–791). Sage.

Honarbin-Holliday, M. (2005). *Art education, identity and gender at Tehran and al Zahra Universities* (PhD thesis). Canterbury Christ Church University, Canterbury.

Honarbin-Holliday, M. (2009). *Becoming visible in Iran: women in contemporary Iranian society.* I B Tauris.

Honarbin-Holliday, M. (2013). Emerging forms of masculinity in the Islamic Republic of Iran. In A. Serberny & M. Torfeh (Eds.), *Cultural revolution in Iran: contemporary popular culture in the Islamic Republic* (pp. 59–77). I B Tauris.

Howatt, A. P. R., & Smith, R. (2014). The history of teaching English as a foreign language, from a British and European perspective. *Language & History,* 57(1), 75–95.

Hughes, K. (2014). The middle classes: etiquette and upward mobility. Discovering Literature: Romantics & Victorians (15th May). Retrieved from https://www.bl.uk/romantics-and-victorians/articles/the-middle-classes-etiquette-and-upward-mobility#

Humberstone, H. B. (1953). *The desert song.* Warner Brothers.

Jabri, V. (2013). *The postcolonial subject: claiming politics/governing others in late modernity.* Routledge.

Jones, E. (2017). Problematising and reimagining the notion of 'international student experience'. *Studies in Higher Education,* 42(5), 933–943.

Kabbani, R. (1986). *Europe's myth of orient: devise and rule.* Macmillan.

Kamal, A. (2015). Interrogating assumptions of native-speakerism from the perspective of Kuwait university English language students. In A. Swan, P. J. Aboshiha, & A. R. Holliday (Eds.), *(En)countering native-speakerism: global perspectives* (pp. 124–140). Palgrave.

Kamali, M. (2019). *The stationery shop of Tehran.* Simon and Schuster.

Kapur, S. (2002). *The four feathers*. Paramount, Miramax.

Kebabi, A. (forthcoming). *'Identity' and 'belonging' in the personal lives of high-status professionals living in the UK: racism, and freedom in material and non-material 'culture'* (PhD thesis). Canterbury Christ Church University, Canterbury, UK.

Kubota, R. (2001). Discursive construction of the images of US classrooms. *TESOL Quarterly*, 35(1), 9–37.

Kubota, R., & Lin, A. M. Y. (2006). Race and TESOL: introduction to concepts and theories. *TESOL Quarterly*, 40(3), 471–493.

Kubota, R., & Lin, A. M. Y. (Eds.). (2009). *Race, culture, and identities in second language education: exploring critically engaged practice*. Routledge.

Kuhn, T. (1970). *The structure of scientific revolutions*. University of Chicago Press.

Kullman, J. (2013). Telling tales: changing discourses of identity in the global UK-published English language coursebook. In J. Gray (Ed.), Critical *perspectives on language teaching materials* (pp. 17–39). Palgrave.

Kumaravadivelu, B. (1993). Maximising learning potential in the communicative classroom. *ELT Journal*, 47(1), 12–21.

Kumaravadivelu, B. (2007). *Cultural globalization and language education*. Yale University Press.

Kunz, S. (2019). Expatriate or migrant? The racialised politics of migration categories and the 'space in-between'. *Discover Society*. Retrieved from https://discoversociety.org/2019/10/02/expatriate-or-migrant-the-racialised-politics-of-migration-categories-and-the-space-in-between/

Lalami, L. (2015). *The Moor's account* (Kindle ed.). Periscope.

Lewis, B. (1982). The question of orientalism. *The New York Review of Books* (June 24th), 1–20. Retrieved from https://www.amherst.edu/media/view/307584/original/The+Question+of+Orientalism+by+Bernard+Lewis+%7C+The+New+York+Review+of+Books.pdf

Lewis, R. (2005). *When cultures collide: Leading across cultures: leading, teamworking and managing across the globe* (3rd ed.). Nicholas Brealey.

Lindholm, T., & Mednick Myles, J. (2017). *Navigating the intercultural classroom*. TESOL Press.

Lowe, R. J. (2020). *Uncovering ideology in English language teaching: identifying the 'native speaker' frame*. Springer.

Lucas, G. (1983). *Star wars: return of the Jedi*. 20th Century Fox.

Lyotard, J.-F. (1979). *The postmodern condition: a report on knowledge* (G. Bennington & B. Massoumi, Trans.). Manchester University Press.

MacDougall, D. (1975). Beyond observational cinema. In P. Hockings (Ed.), *Principles of visual anthropology* (pp. 109–125). Mouton.

Macpherson, W. (1999). *The Stephen Lawrence enquiry: report of an enquiry*. UK Government.

Mahboob, A. (2015). Language has no ethnicity. *Tribune*, December 12th.

Mami, F. (2014). Circumventing cultural reification: A study of Chimamanda Ngozi Adichie's *The thing around your neck*. *Romanian Journal of English Studies*, 11(1) 215–225.

Mannheim, K. (1936). *Ideology and utopia.* Harcourt, Brace & Company.

Martindale, D. (1960). *The nature and types of sociological theory.* Routledge & Kegan Paul.

Marx Knoetze, H. (2004). Archetypes of memory and amnesia in South African soap opera. *Tydskirf vir Letterkunde,* 41(4), 113–126.

Marx Knoetze, H. (2018). Who feels at home? Whiteness and the politics of belonging in the Flemish soap opera Thuis. *Critical Arts, South-North Cultural and Media Studies,* 32(2), 48–66.

Mason, A. E. W. (1902). *The four feathers.* Macmillan.

Mauss, M. (1973/1935). Techniques of the body. *Economy and Society,* 2(1), 70–88.

Mernissi, F. (2001). *Scheherazade goes West: different cultures, different harems.* Washington Square Press.

Mills, C. W. (1959/1970). *The sociological imagination.* Pelican.

Munby, J. (1978). *Communicative syllabus design: a sociolinguistic model for defining the content of purpose-specific language programmes.* Cambridge University Press.

Nour, E. (2020). *The stray cats of Homs* (E. Broom, Trans.).

Ogden, T. H. (2004). The analytic third: implications for psychoanalytic theory and technique. *Psychoanalytic Quarterly,* 73, 167–195.

Osmond, J., & Roed, J. (2009). Sometimes it means more work... In E. Jones (Ed.), *Internationalisation and the student voice: higher education perspectives* (pp. 113–124). Routledge.

Oukraf, A. (forthcoming). *Resilience construction among international PhD students: learning from Facebook posts, daily practices and creative nonfiction* (PhD thesis). Canterbury Christ Church University, Canterbury.

Padula, A. (2009). Kinesics. In *encyclopedia of communication theory* (pp. 582–584). Sage.

Pennycook, A. (1998). *English and the discourses of colonialism.* Routledge.

Pennycook, A., & Makoni, N. (2020). *Innovations and challenges in applied linguistics from the Global South.* Routledge.

Phillipson, R. (1992). *Linguistic imperialism.* Oxford University Press.

Ploner, J., & Jones, L. (2019). Learning to belong? 'Culture' and 'place making' among children and young people in Hull, UK City of Culture 2017. *Children's Geographies,* 1–14.

Popper, K. (1966a). *The open society and its enemies: Volume 1, Plato.* Routledge and Kegan Paul.

Popper, K. (1966b). *The open society and its enemies: Volume 2, Hegel and Marx.* Routledge and Kegan Paul.

Rajagopalan, K. (2012). Colonial hangover and the new 'hybrid' Englishes. In R. K. Agnihotri & R. Singh (Eds.), *Indian English: towards a new paradigm* (pp. 206–215). Orient Black Swan.

Risager, K. (2020). Linguaculture and transnationality. In J. Jackson (Ed.), *Routledge handbook of language and intercultural communication* (pp. 109–123). Routledge.

Rixon, S., & Smith, R. (2012). The work of Brian Abbs and Ingrid Freebairn. *ELT Journal,* 66(3), 383–393.

Ros i Solé, C. (2019). Re-visiting the unhomely through languaging. *Language and Intercultural Communication*, 19(1), 38–50.

Rostami-Povey, E. (2007). *Afghan women: identity and invasion*. Zed Books.

Ryan, J., & Louie, K. (2007). False dichotomy? 'Western' and 'Confucian' concepts of scholarship and learning. *Educational Philosophy & Theory*, 39(4), 404–417.

Sadoudi, Y. (forthcoming). *'Travelling to the West': voices of Algerian PhD students' transition to Britain* (PhD thesis). Canterbury Christ Church University, Canterbury, UK.

Saheb-e Zamani, N. (1972). *Tha third script: personality, sayings and thoughts of Shams-e Tabrizi*. The Atai Press.

Said, E. (1978). *Orientalism*. Routledge & Kegan Paul.

Said, E., & Grabar, O. (1982). Orientalism: an exchange. *The New York Review of Books* (August 12th). Retrieved from https://www.nybooks.com/articles/1982/08/12/orientalism-an-exchange/

Saraceni, M. (2015). *World Englishes: a critical analysis*. Bloomsbury.

Schneider, E. W. (2016). Hybrid Englishes: An exploratory survey. *World Englishes*, 35(3), 339–354.

Schudson, M. (1994). Culture and the integration of national societies. In D. Crane (Ed.), *The sociology of culture* (pp. 21–43). Blackwell.

Schutz, A. (1944). The stranger: an essay in social psychology. *American Journal of Sociology*, 49(9), 499–507.

Shafak, E. (2010). *Forty rules of love*. Viking.

Shahraz, Q. (2013). *The holy woman* (Kindle ed.). Arcadia Books.

Simmel, G. (1903). The sociology of conflict I. *American Journal of Sociology*, 9, 490–525.

Simmel, G. (1908/1950). *The stranger* (K. Wolff, Trans.). In K. Wolff (Ed.), *The sociology of George Simmel* (pp. 402–408). Free Press.

Soja, E. W. (1996). *Thirdspace: journeys to Los Angeles and other real-and-imagined places*. Wiley-Blackwell.

Souleh, N. E. (forthcoming). *Exploring Othering with intersectional feminist aspirations: between lived experiences and stand-up comedy* (PhD thesis). Canterbury Christ Church University, Canterbury, UK.

Spears, A. K. (Ed.) (1999). *Race and ideology; language, symbolism, and popular culture*. Wayne State University Press.

Spencer-Oatey, H. (2000). Introduction: language, culture and rapport management. In H. Spencer-Oatey (Ed.), *Culturally speaking: managing rapport through talk across cultures* (pp. 1–8). Continuum.

Stone, O. (2004). *Alexander*. Warner Brothers Pictures.

Triandis, H. C. (1995). *Individualism and collectivism*. Westview Press.

UNESCO. (2010). UNESCO universal declaration on cultural diversity: Adopted by the 31st Session of the General Conference of UNESCO Paris, 2nd November. UNESCO.

Weber, M. (1905/1950). *The Protestant ethic and the spirit of capitalism* (T. Parsons, Trans. 3rd ed.). George Allen & Unwin.

Weber, M. (1922/1964). *The theory of social and economic organisation*. The Free Press.

Weber, M. (1949/1968). Ideal types and theory construction. In M. Brodbeck (Ed.), *Readings in the philosophy of the social sciences* (pp. 496–507). Macmillan.

Wenger, E. (2000). Communities of practice and social learning systems. *Organization*, 7(2), 225–246.

Williams, C. (2020). *Some new world: report on British Council Fellowship to the Venice Biennale*. Unpublished paper. Canterbury Christ Church University. Canterbury.

Wodak, R. (2008). 'Us and them': inclusion and exclusion. In G. Delanty, R. Wodak, & P. Jones (Eds.), *Identity, belonging and migration* (pp. 54–77). Liverpool University Press.

Wodak, R., & Meyer, M. (2015). Critical discourse studies: history, agenda, theory and methodology. In R. Wodak & M. Meyer (Eds.), *Methods or critical discourse studies* (3rd ed., pp. 2–22). Sage.

Worsley, W., & von Fritsch, G. (1954). *Flash Gordon*. DuMont Television Network.

Wu, B. (2021). *Staging international student mobility: an ethnography of precarity, negotiation and agency of African students at a Chinese university* (PhD thesis). Canterbury Christ Church University, Canterbury, UK.

Wu, Z. (2015). Making the past speak again: practicing heritage across cultural boundaries. Paper presented at the International Association of Language & Intercultural Communication Annual Conference, Intercultural Communication in Social Practice, Peking University.

Yamchi, N. (2015). 'I am not what you think I am': EFL undergraduates' experience of academic writing, facing discourses of formulaic writing. In A. Swan, P. J. Aboshiha, & A. R. Holliday (Eds.), *(En)countering native-speakerism: global perspectives* (pp. 177–192). Palgrave.

Zaharin, I. (2020). *Radical change in appearance, religiousness, language and openness amongst a small group of Malaysian students: rethinking the intercultural* (PhD thesis). Canterbury Christ Church University, Canterbury.

Index